O8120

rning Exchange

The Social Worker's Guide to the Mental Capacity Act 2005

F

Post-qualifying Social Work Practice – other titles in the series

To order, please contact our distributor: BEBC Distribution, Albion Close, Parkstone, Poole, BH12 3LL. Telephone: 0845 230 9000, email: **learningmatters@bebc.co.uk.**

You can also find more information on each of these titles and our other learning resources at **www.learningmatters.co.uk.**

The Social Worker's Guide to the Mental Capacity Act 2005

ROBERT BROWN

PAUL BARBER

Series Editor: Keith Brown

LearningMatters

First published in 2008 by Learning Matters Ltd
Reprinted in 2008

British Library Cataloguing in Publication Data
A CIP record for this book is available from the British Library.

ISBN: 978 184445 129 6

Cover and text design by Code 5 Design Associates Ltd
Project Management by Swales & Willis Ltd
Typeset by RefineCatch Limited, Bungay, Suffolk
Printed and bound in Great Britain by TJ International Ltd, Padstow, Cornwall

Learning Matters Ltd
33 Southernhay East
Exeter EX1 1 NX
Tel: 01392 215560
info@learningmatters.co.uk
www.learningmatters.co.uk

Contents

Foreword from the Series Editor

This is a very timely and important text as the Mental Capacity Act 2005 affects all social work practice with people over the age of 16 who may lack capacity in relation to any decision.

Robert Brown and Paul Barber have written this text in a style which is accessible to all professionals, and their detailed knowledge and experience of working in this field is very apparent. All social workers need to be aware of the Mental Capacity Act 2005 and its implications for their practice and this text clearly spells out these implications. All social workers would be wise to have a copy of this text close to hand to help inform their practice.

I warmly commend to all professionals this text, which, together with the two companion texts – *The Approved Social Worker's Guide to Mental Health Law* and *The Approved Social Worker's Guide to Psychiatry and Medication* – make a valuable contribution to the development of the best possible social work practice in our society.

Keith Brown
Director of Centre for Post-qualifying Social Work
Bournemouth University
4th Floor, Royal London House
Christchurch Road
Bournemouth BH1 3LT

About the authors

Robert Brown is Director of the Approved Social Workers course in south-west England, delivered in association with Bournemouth University. He is also the Area Mental Health Act Commissioner for Dorset and Somerset and has lectured at Southampton University, Stirling University and Croydon College. Rob has published widely in the field of mental health law.

Paul Barber qualified in 1976 and is a former partner at Bevan Ashford Solicitors (now Bevan Brittan) where for many years he led the firm's NHS Litigation Department. Paul now works as a consultant to the firm and is involved with training Approved Social Workers and lecturing on Section 12 Approval courses for doctors. Paul also provides training for the Mental Health Act Commission.

Preface

Welcome to the *Social Worker's Guide to the Mental Capacity Act 2005*. This book has been designed primarily for qualified social workers but it should also be useful for those on social work courses, other health professionals, service users, carers and others interested in the fields of mental health, physical health, learning disability and old age. The law as described relates to England and Wales. Note that the law is significantly different in Scotland, in Northern Ireland and in the Channel Islands.

There are two companion texts in this series. *The Approved Social Worker's Guide to Mental Health Law* is issued to many trainee and practising ASWs. It covers mental health law in some detail, and the second edition considers the relationship between mental health and mental capacity law. There is significant potential overlap between these two areas of law. There is also *The Approved Social Worker's Guide to Psychiatry and Medication*. This book contains a brief summary of current law in both areas in so far as they affect treatment for mental disorder.

With the exception of the 'Bournewood' provisions the Mental Capacity Act has been operational since October 2007 in England and Wales. The 'Bournewood' provisions cover people who lack capacity to make a decision about being in hospitals, nursing homes or care homes in situations which amount to deprivation of liberty. This part of the Act is not expected to come into effect until April 2009 but it is included in this book in a separate chapter in anticipation of this event. There is also an appendix which summarises the new proposals.

The Mental Capacity Act 2005 takes, adapts and clothes in statutory form a number of areas of common (judge made) law, in particular:

- the test for incapacity;

- the means of establishing 'best interests';

- the authority to intervene in relation to a person lacking capacity and the limits to that authority;

- the law relating to advance decisions.

Just when the common law will continue to apply in relation to dealing with those lacking capacity is an interesting issue and outside the scope of this book. What is left of the common law will depend to some extent upon how the courts construe the Mental

Capacity Act, whether broadly or narrowly. Perhaps the safest advice would be to confine the use of common law powers in relation to a person lacking capacity to emergencies and short-term interventions.

This book is not just aimed at Approved Social Workers, because the Mental Capacity Act 2005 affects all social workers who are dealing with anyone over the age of 16 who may lack capacity in relation to any decisions. This long-awaited Act should assist staff in these circumstances. Hopefully this book will make the law accessible and understandable to a wide range of practitioners.

At the end of each chapter we have included key points and questions, sometimes in multiple choice form, in an attempt to aid learning. Some of the most important points are then summarised in Appendices to try and help busy practitioners.

We would like to thank Tracy Gallagher, Anthony Harbour and Debbie Martin who read and commented on this book when it was in its draft form. Their views, based on their experience and knowledge of how the law operates within social work practice, have been very helpful to us. However, we accept responsibility for any inaccuracies which remain within the text.

Robert Brown, South West ASW Programme Director and
Paul Barber, Consultant, Bevan Brittan, Solicitors

c/o Institute of Health and Community Studies, Post-qualifying Social Work Team, Bournemouth University, 4th Floor, Royal London House, Christchurch Road, Bournemouth, BH1 3LT.

Chapter 1

Background to the Mental Capacity Act 2005

Introduction

The Mental Capacity Act, as passed in 2005 and implemented in 2007, is the culmination of more than fifteen years of work. Before making a detailed examination of the provisions of the Act it is worth placing it in context by looking briefly at the events which led to the Act reaching the statute book.

The Law Society (1989) had highlighted some difficulties in a paper published prior to the conference on 'Decision making and Mental Incapacity'. This led to the involvement of the Law Commission (1991) which published Consultation Paper No. 119 entitled 'Mentally Incapacitated Adults and Decision-Making: An Overview'. Para 1.9 of the Law Commission paper clearly stated why new law was needed:

> The existing law relating to decision-making on behalf of mentally incapacitated adults is fragmented, complex and in many respects out of date. There is no coherent concept of their status, and there are many gaps where the law provides no effective mechanism for resolving problems. Debate, stimulated by a series of High Court decisions on sterilisation and abortion, has recently focused on the obtaining of consent to serious medical procedures, but the problems extend far beyond this issue.

The Consultation Paper identified a number of problem areas involving capacity and decision-making. These included:

- consent to medical treatment;

- disputes between relatives;

- significant life decisions. Where an adult was not capable of making decisions such as whether to continue living at home, it was not clear who had ultimate responsibility for making such a decision;

- suspicions of abuse or neglect. There were problems deciding at what stage intervention was justified and who should be responsible for taking any action;

- young people leaving care. Those with a mental incapacity might not be eligible for guardianship under the Mental Health Act 1983 and yet neither foster parents nor local authority would have any continuing legal responsibility under child care law.

Prior to the passing of the Mental Capacity Act there was a variety of legislation which was relevant to these issues but, as noted above, it was fragmented, complex and out of date.

Key issues to be resolved

There are some tensions which the law may be asked to deal with. Maximising freedom and autonomy may conflict with a need for care or control. Again, protection from abuse or exploitation may involve some invasion of a person's autonomy. Another issue is how to identify an acceptable level of risk for an individual. If a professional intervenes without a clear legal base and guidance, they lay themselves open to allegations of undue influence or misconduct. If they do not intervene, they may be accused of neglecting their duty of care. Finally, not intervening may result in other people being harmed or in suffering in some way. If the person causing the harm is seen as 'mentally incapacitated', this raises the question whether they should face the full penalty of law (e.g. through a criminal or civil action) or whether they should be dealt with differently because of their lack of understanding of the consequences of their actions.

The concept of mental capacity

There is a distinction to be drawn between a legal definition of capacity (or incapacity) and medical or psychological definitions, though on occasions they will be the same. Para 2.10 of the 1991 paper stated:

> *A legal incapacity arises whenever the law provides that a particular person is incapable of taking a particular decision, undertaking a particular juristic act, or engaging in a particular activity. Incapacity can arise from a variety of conditions; historically, these included being under the age of majority, or a married woman, or of unsound mind. Under the modern law, a great many different approaches have developed to the question of capacity based on mental state. Generally there is a presumption that the person is capable until proved otherwise, and capacity is judged in relation to the particular decision, transaction or activity involved. There is also a basic common law test of capacity, to the effect that the person concerned must at the relevant time understand in broad terms what he is doing and the likely effects of his action. Thus, in principle, legal capacity depends upon understanding rather than wisdom: the quality of the decision is irrelevant as long as the person understands what he is deciding.*

This approach to the definition of mental incapacity was broadly followed in the 2005 Act as will be seen when we examine the provisions in detail.

The work of the Law Commission

There were four consultation papers before the Law Commission (1995) published its final report. This comprehensive document included a Draft Mental Incapacity Bill. The proposal, which has broadly been revived by the 2005 Act, was to introduce a new Act, which would be separate from the Mental Health Act 1983, and which would provide a coherent statutory framework for decision-making for those who lacked capacity. The two key issues were capacity and best interests, and these are at the heart of the 2005 Act. A new Court of Protection would be created to provide a statutory jurisdiction for making a range of decisions on behalf of people who lacked capacity.

It is unfortunate that these proposals were stalled by the then Government's decision not to proceed. A proposed consultation on the report did not materialise. Ashton et al. (2006) attribute the Government's reaction to a defensive response to an attack on the Law Commission by the *Daily Mail* in support of family values. Living wills in particular came in for criticism. There were some echoes of these issues in the criticisms of the 2005 Act in its final stages as a Bill.

Who decides?

This Green Paper was published by the Lord Chancellor (1997). It contained recommendations for defining incapacity, providing a framework for carers, giving more powers to the Court of Protection, introducing new powers of attorney. It also considered the issue of costs and whether the expense of any new legislation would be worthwhile.

Making decisions

The Lord Chancellor's proposals were contained in this 1999 report. Many of these proposals would find their way into the 2005 Act:

- a new functional test of capacity;
- a best interests approach to decision-making;
- a reformed Court of Protection with a regional presence and powers to make single issues orders or to appoint someone to manage decisions for someone who lacked capacity;
- continuing powers of attorney.

Despite this revival of key elements of the Law Commission's proposals there was still a wait for parliamentary time and it was another four years before a Bill was published.

The Mental Incapacity Bill

A draft Mental Incapacity Bill was published in 2003. (This was three years after Scotland passed its own Adults With Incapacity (Scotland) Act 2000. A discussion of the Scottish Act can be found in Ashton (2006)). The Draft Mental Incapacity Bill was scrutinised by a Joint Committee of both Houses of Parliament. This led to a number of changes including:

- a change in the title from 'Incapacity' to 'Capacity';

- a statement of principles to be included;

- refinements to the proposals for Lasting Powers of Attorney;

- standards of professional conduct to be included in the Codes of Practice.

The Committee also considered that the Bill should receive priority and then influence mental health law. The amended Bill was introduced in Parliament in June 2004 and passed in April 2005 just before the General Election.

Despite some late alarms the Bill just managed to complete its passage before Parliament was dissolved and at last England and Wales were to have a statutory response to difficult issues of decision-making where persons over the age of 16 lacked the capacity to make decisions for themselves. In many ways it is a radical and innovative Act and it will be of great interest to see if it is viewed as a success in terms of improving legal support for some very vulnerable individuals.

Chapter 2
The key features of the Mental Capacity Act 2005

Introduction

In this chapter we provide an overview of the main provisions of the Mental Capacity Act and consider how the Act should work in practice. This will be followed by a chapter on the Code of Practice. The rest of the book looks at the Act in more depth. The text of the main body of the Act is provided at the end of the book for reference purposes (pages 102–38).

This chapter can therefore serve as a quick introduction to the essential elements of the Mental Capacity Act 2005, or it can serve as a revision tool for those who are more familiar with the Act's provisions.

The Mental Capacity Act provides a statutory framework for decision-making for persons over the age of 16 who are incapable of making certain decisions for themselves. The Act does not prescribe who the decision-maker should be in every circumstance, and the guidance on this issue in the Code of Practice is very limited although it does provide a mechanism for resolving any disputes in this area. A significant part of the Act is devoted to setting out the procedures that should be followed in making any such decisions. It covers a broad range of decisions including personal welfare decisions, medical and healthcare decisions, as well as financial decisions. To a significant extent many well-established common law principles are enshrined within the Act.

We will now summarise the key features of the Act.

The five principles

In stark contrast with the Mental Health Act 1983 (which starts with a definition of mental disorder) the Mental Capacity Act begins by establishing five key principles to be followed whenever working within the framework of the Act. These are:

1. A person must be assumed to have capacity unless it is established that he lacks capacity.

2. A person is not to be treated as unable to make a decision unless all practicable steps to help him to do so have been taken without success.

3. A person is not to be treated as unable to make a decision merely because he makes an unwise decision.

4. An act done, or decision made, under this Act for or on behalf of a person who lacks capacity must be done, or made, in his best interests.

5. Before the act is done, or the decision is made, regard must be had to whether the purpose for which it is needed can be as effectively achieved in a way that is less restrictive of the person's rights and freedom of action.

These principles will be considered in more depth in Chapter 4.

Mental incapacity defined

Section (s) 2 of the Act states that for the purposes of the Act:

> *a person lacks capacity in relation to a matter if at the material time he is unable to make a decision for himself in relation to the matter because of an impairment of, or a disturbance in the functioning of, the mind or brain.*

This is referred to as the 'diagnostic test'. This broad definition, which might catch so many people, is effectively cut down by application of the 'functional test' so that only the smallest area of decision-making necessary is identified for application of the incapacity test.

Section 3 then provides the test that should be used. It is an interesting development of tests that had been established by the courts such as in the case of C *(Adult: Refusal of Medical Treatment)* 1994. The s 3 test is that:

> *a person is unable to make a decision for himself if he is unable –*
>
> *(a) to understand the information relevant to the decision,*
>
> *(b) to retain that information,*
>
> *(c) to use or weigh that information as part of the process of making the decision, or*
>
> *(d) to communicate his decision (whether by talking, using sign language or any other means).*

An inability to satisfy any one of these four conditions would render the person incapable. Chapter 5 looks at the functional approach to defining mental incapacity, offers a checklist for assessment and considers the issue of how to record any assessments of capacity.

Best interests

Section 2 of the Act states that a person making a decision with regard to someone who lacks capacity must, in determining their best interests, take the following steps. These, in effect, are a checklist which is set out in s 4 of the Act. This is considered in more depth in Chapter 6 but, in summary, the decision maker must:

- consider whether it is likely that the person will at some time have capacity in relation to the matter in question;

- permit and encourage the person to participate as fully as possible in any act done for him and any decision affecting him;

- consider the person's past and present wishes and feelings (and, in particular, any relevant written statement made by him when he had capacity);

- consider the beliefs and values that would be likely to influence his decision if he had capacity, and the other factors that he would be likely to consider if he were able to do so;

- take into account, if it is practicable and appropriate to consult them, the views of:

  - anyone named by the person as someone to be consulted on the matter in question or on matters of that kind;

  - anyone engaged in caring for the person or interested in his welfare;

  - any donee of a Lasting Power of Attorney granted by the person; and

  - any deputy appointed for the person by the court,

  as to what would be in the person's best interests.

It is important to note that in the case of an act done, or a decision made, by a person other than the court, there is sufficient compliance with this section if (having complied with this checklist) he reasonably believes that what he does or decides is in the best interests of the person concerned. Chapter 6 describes the Act's approach to determining best interests.

Protection for those making decisions

One of the essential features of the Mental Capacity Act is the protection it offers to anyone who makes a decision after applying the requirements of the Act. In essence, if a person does something in connection with the care or treatment of another person, they are protected if, before doing the act, they take reasonable steps to establish whether that person lacks capacity in relation to the matter in question, and, when doing the act, reasonably believe that the person lacks capacity in relation to the matter, and that it will be in their best interests for the act to be done. In many situations people will find it appropriate to make a clear record of this process and some NHS Trusts and local authorities have produced guidance for this. For ease of access the 'best interests checklist' is set out at Appendix 4. Professional staff might wish to ensure that any local proformas meet the statutory requirements by checking them against this list to ensure that all points have been covered.

If a decision-maker follows the Act's requirements it would, in effect, be as if the incapacitated person had had capacity and had made the decision themselves. This protection will be of no value, however, if the person has not followed the best interests checklist or has acted negligently. Chapter 7 looks at the relevant sub-section (ss) 5–8 in some detail.

Lasting Powers of Attorney

A Lasting Power of Attorney is a power of attorney under which the donor (who must be 18 or over) confers on the donee (or donees) (sometimes referred to as an attorney) authority to make decisions about all or any of their personal welfare matters or their property and affairs, and which includes authority to make such decisions in circumstances where P no longer has capacity. ('P' is used in the Act to define the person whose capacity is in question, and 'D' is used to define the person who does an act in respect of 'P'. See s 5.) Personal welfare could include health or social matters.

This is a form of substituted decision-making. These powers are dealt with in Chapter 8. From 1 October 2007 no new Enduring Powers of Attorney can be made. They are replaced by Lasting Powers of Attorney (LPAs) which may be either a property and affairs LPA or a personal welfare LPA. If a person wishes to cover both areas of decision-making then separate LPAs will be required. EPAs made before 1 October 2007 will still be valid but will be limited to property and affairs.

Deputies and declarations

If a person lacks capacity in relation to a matter either of personal welfare or property and affairs, the court may make the decision on the person's behalf in relation to the matter, or the court could appoint a deputy to make decisions on the person's behalf in relation to the matter or matters. Again, this is sometimes referred to as 'substituted decision-making'. The court will start from the presumption that it will make the decision itself but there will be some complex cases involving a series of decisions where it may be seen as more appropriate to appoint a deputy. This is considered in more detail in Chapter 9.

In addition, as a branch of the High Court of Justice the Court of Protection has power to make declarations as to whether a person has or lacks capacity to make certain decisions. It would be appropriate to ask the court for a declaration in circumstances where, despite following the procedures set out in the Act and the guidance contained in the Code of Practice, the decision-maker found it impossible to reach a conclusion as to whether the person had capacity or not. It would not be appropriate to ask for a declaration simply to give reassurance for a decision that was fairly clear.

Declarations could also be made with regard to the lawfulness or otherwise of any act done, or to be done, in relation to a person.

Advance decisions

This part of the Act only covers people aged 18 or over.

Advance decisions to refuse treatment, sometimes referred to as 'living wills', 'advance directives' or 'advance refusals' have long been recognised within common law. An adult of sound mind is entitled to refuse medical treatment, whether face to face with the healthcare professional, or in advance, anticipating a time when the person may lack capacity to refuse the treatment in question.

The Mental Capacity Act codifies this law and adds a requirement that for life-sustaining treatment issues the advance decision should be in writing and witnessed. For other treatments there is no such requirement but the refusal needs to be seen as valid and applicable in the particular circumstances which present themselves. Chapter 10 covers this issue in some depth.

Independent Mental Capacity Advocates (IMCAs)

In England this aspect of the Act was introduced in April 2007. In Wales it was not introduced until the rest of the Act was implemented in October 2007. The IMCA scheme was piloted in a number of areas before the Act was passed.

Where serious medical treatment or a change of residence is proposed for a person who lacks capacity in relation to the decision, and where that person has no family or friends whom it is appropriate to consult, an IMCA must be appointed.

The advocate should take such steps as are necessary to support the person they have been instructed to represent so that the person may participate as fully as possible in any relevant decision. They should also:

- obtain and evaluate relevant information;
- find out what the person's wishes and feelings would be likely to be;
- ascertain the beliefs and values that would be likely to influence the person if they had capacity;
- explore what alternative courses of action are available;
- obtain a further medical opinion where treatment is proposed and the advocate thinks that one should be obtained.

The Mental Capacity Act 2005 (Independent Mental Capacity Advocates) (General) Regulations (2006, No. 1832) which accompany the Act also make provision as to circumstances in which an advocate may challenge, or provide assistance for the purpose of challenging, any relevant decision.

Social workers should ensure that they know how to contact the IMCA scheme in relevant circumstances. The circumstances in which IMCAs could (as opposed to must) become involved has also been expanded. Chapter 11 looks at IMCAs.

The Court of Protection and the Public Guardian

The Court of Protection is a far more powerful and wide-ranging body in its powers and scope than the Court as it was established under the Mental Health Act. Chapter 12 describes the Court's structure. It will deal with all issues concerning people who lack capacity, not merely making orders in respect of their property and affairs but in addition covering issues of personal welfare including the making of medical decisions. Most decisions will be made without recourse to the Court but some examples of when the Court would be involved are:

- where the cumulative restrictions or restraints imposed upon a person who lacked capacity amounted to a deprivation of liberty and therefore could not lawfully be imposed as a section 5 act;

- where there were genuine concerns about the manner in which an attorney or a deputy was acting (for example apparently ignoring the best interests checklist);

- where there was doubt over the meaning or construction of an LPA or whether an advance decision was valid or applicable;

- where it was felt that there might be the need for a deputy to be appointed.

There are more examples set out in Chapter 12.

The gateway to the Court of Protection is a new body, the Public Guardian, appointed by the Lord Chancellor. The functions of the Public Guardian include:

- establishing and maintaining registers of LPAs and court appointed-deputies;

- supervising deputies;

- directing Court of Protection Visitors to visit and report on LPA attorneys, deputies or the person lacking capacity.

Other issues

There are a number of other aspects to the Mental Capacity Act which are summarised in the last four chapters. The introduction of new offences connected with ill-treatment or neglect of a person should help to strengthen vulnerable adults procedures.

There are some areas that are specifically excluded from the scope of the Act and these are identified in Chapter 13.

There are significant new safeguards and procedural safeguards with regard to research involving people who lack the capacity to consent to take part. These are listed in Chapter 14.

Chapter 15 considers the relationship of the Mental Capacity Act with other legislation such as the Human Rights Act 1998 and the Mental Health Act 1983.

Finally the 'Bournewood' provisions are outlined in Chapter 16. These provisions were added to the Act by the Mental Health Act 2007 to cover the situation of the person who is mentally incapable of deciding whether to be in a hospital, nursing home or care home, but who is in effect deprived of his liberty. This part of the Act is not yet in force which is why it is covered in a final separate chapter.

The Act is reprinted at the end of the book for easy access. This does not include all of the Schedules to the Act. The book also has several appendices which provide some quick and easy guides to working under the Act. These also include the answers to the multiple choice questions which appear at the end of some chapters (starting with this one) to help consolidate knowledge of the material.

ACTIVITY 2.1

Multiple choice questions

Read each question carefully and tick the appropriate box(es). Where a statement is correct, tick the box next to it; if it is incorrect, leave it blank. You may need to tick more than one box per question.

Appendix 5 (pages 145–9) gives the answers.

2.1 *The Mental Capacity Act 2005:*

(a) *Places advance decisions relating to treatment on a statutory footing*

(b) *Defines incapacity*

(c) *Retains the current common law test for capacity to consent to treatment, without change*

(d) *Introduces substituted decision-making in relation to healthcare matters*

(e) *Regulates research relating to incapacitated persons*

(f) *Fills the 'Bournewood gap' by allowing deputies to authorise deprivation of liberty*

2.2 *The Mental Capacity Act contains a checklist which determines who should be the decision maker in any specified situation:*

(a) *True*

(b) *False*

2.3 *Under the Mental Capacity Act someone may be appointed under a Lasting Power of Attorney to make healthcare decisions for a person when he/she becomes incapacitated:*

(a) *True*

(b) *False*

2.4 *To be protected when doing anything under 5 of the Act a person must:*

(a) *establish that the person lacks capacity in relation to the matter in question*

(b) *notify the Public Guardian of the decision if it incurs significant costs*

(c) *believe that the action will be in the person's best interests*

(d) *obtain medical evidence of mental incapacity*

(e) *inform the nearest relative of any action taken*

Chapter 3
The Code of Practice
(sections 42–43)

Introduction

The Code of Practice came into effect in April 2007 to coincide with those provisions of the Act which were introduced at that time, namely the Independent Mental Capacity Advocacy Service for England and the section 44 criminal offence of ill-treatment or neglect of a person lacking capacity. In the time between April and the remaining sections of the Act coming into force in October 2007, ss 1–4 of the Act which deal with the statutory principles, the definition and assessment of capacity, and determining best interests needed to be applied when the IMCA service was involved. As a result the Code of Practice guidance in relation to these sections was in place to be referred to by those covered by it on such occasions. Fortunately this twin-track approach was short-lived and, it is to be hoped, will not have created too much confusion in the meantime. Given that the Code of Practice is founded on good professional practice, health and social care professionals will not have gone far wrong during this period in following its guidance in relation to these sections whether or not an IMCA was involved.

What does the Code of Practice cover?

Section 42(1) sets out what the code or codes must cover, including:

- guidance for people assessing capacity;
- guidance for people performing s 5 acts (i.e. acts in connection with the care or treatment of a person lacking capacity);
- guidance for people appointed as attorneys under LPAs;
- guidance for deputies appointed by the Court of Protection;
- guidance for people carrying out research covered by ss 30–34 of the Act;
- guidance for Independent Mental Capacity Advocates;
- guidance in relation to advance decisions covered by ss 24–26;
- guidance in relation to such other matters concerned with the Act as the Lord Chancellor sees fit.

It would seem that those charged with drawing up the Code have construed their obligations broadly as there are substantial chapters in relation to:

- the position of children and young people, whether under this Act or the Children Act or indeed the Mental Health Act (Chapter 12);

- the informal and formal resolution of disputes, whether between health and social care professionals or health and social care professionals and others (Chapter 15);

- the interface between the Mental Capacity Act and the Mental Health Act (Chapter 13); and

- the rules governing access to information about a person who lacks capacity (Chapter 16).

In these chapters the Code of Practice resembles less a paraphrase of the Act (which is its tendency elsewhere) than a useful and informed commentary on its context. The Code is eminently readable, indeed almost chatty and far removed in style from the current (though perhaps not future) Code of Practice relating to the Mental Health Act, including many examples and case studies within the text to illustrate the practice points being made. As a result it is quite long, running to some 300 pages and is rather bulky for health and social care professionals to carry around with them at work for reference. It is also available on-line from the Ministry of Justice's website (formerly the Department for Constitutional Affairs). Despite its length there are parts which would justify considerable expansion, where potential problems in practice can be anticipated. An example would be the identification of the decision-maker in relation to the assessment of capacity and the determination of best interests, particularly in areas where there a large number of different stakeholders in the decision and outcome. This is an issue on which the Act is virtually silent, and the advice in the Code of Practice is all too brief. Paragraph 5.8 identifies a few simple examples but in practice this is an area where difficulties can be expected.

To whom does the Code of Practice apply?

Section 42(4) sets out that a person is under a duty to have regard to the Code of Practice if acting in relation to a person who lacks capacity in one or more of the following ways:

- as an attorney under a Lasting Power of Attorney;

- as a deputy appointed by the Court of Protection;

- as a person carrying out research covered by ss 30–34;

- as an Independent Mental Capacity Advocate;

- in a professional capacity;

- for remuneration.

As the Code of Practice itself points out in its introduction, the last two categories cover a wide range of individuals. Those acting in a professional capacity would include: healthcare staff such as doctors, dentists, nurses, therapists, radiologists, paramedics, etc.; social care staff such as social workers, care managers, etc.; and others *who may occasionally be involved in the care of people who lack capacity to make the decision in question, such as ambulance crew, housing workers, or police officers.*

It would also include solicitors and other professionals. Those acting for remuneration would include:

care assistants in a care home, care workers providing domiciliary care services, and others who have been contracted to provide a service to people who lack capacity to consent to that service.

These are the people the Act requires to 'have regard' to the Code of Practice. However, the Act itself applies to anyone who is acting in respect of or making a decision for someone who lacks capacity, including those doing so informally. So the Code urges them too to follow its guidance as far as they are aware of it. This may be little more than wishful thinking but non professionals may be able to obtain advice from the Office of the Public Guardian, or from the booklet designed with them in mind by the Mental Capacity Implementation programme available at **www.dca.gov.uk/legal-policy/mental-capacity/publications.htm**.

In respect of recording assessments of capacity and best interests the Code advises:

- assessments (particularly by informal carers) of capacity to take day-to-day decisions do not require recorded documentation (4.60);

- paid carers should keep a record of steps taken (4.60);

- assessments of capacity by professionals in relation to particular decisions should be recorded (4.61);

- staff involved in providing care should make sure a record is kept of the process of working out best interests for each relevant decision and it would be useful for family and other carers to keep a similar record of major decisions (5.15);

- if the decision-maker is not following the written wishes of the person now lacking capacity the reasons must be recorded (5.43).

In practice a care plan incorporating the regular day-to-day decisions and actions taken for a person assessed as lacking capacity to make them will be recorded as having been tested against the best interests checklist, thereby giving protection to staff implementing them. This is subject to the need to be aware that the person may regain capacity to make some at least of those decisions for himself, and that decisions outside those recorded in the care plan will need a separate assessment. This at least is the implication of the rather sparse guidance contained in 5.11 and 4.61.

In the foreword to the Code of Practice Lord Falconer states that the Mental Capacity Act will make a real difference to the lives of people who may lack mental capacity. It will

empower people to make decisions for themselves wherever possible, and protect people who lack capacity by providing a flexible framework that places individuals at the very heart of the decision-making process. It will ensure that they participate as much as possible in any decisions made on their behalf, and that these are made in their best interests. It also allows people to plan ahead for a time in the future when they might lack the capacity, for any number of reasons, to make decisions for themselves.

One of the problems inherent in an Act which aspires to promote a new culture in relation to decision-making for people who lack capacity is that of ensuring that its provisions are made known not simply to health and social care professionals but to all who may be involved, including those caring as best they can and with the best of intentions for a relative who lacks capacity living with them in their home. The existence of an eminently readable and sensible Code of Practice, not to mention the useful booklets published by the Mental Capacity Implementation Programme for different categories of people who might be involved with people who lack capacity, and the availability of so much material on the Ministry of Justice's website will not by themselves ensure that the Act's aims and requirements reach everyone concerned. It is likely to be a number of years and to require a process of direct education of those caring for people who lack capacity by those working in the community who come into contact with them, before the full impact of the Act will be felt.

What is the status and effect of the Code?

As stated above, certain categories of people are required to 'have regard' to the Code of Practice when acting in relation to people who lack capacity. It is interesting to note that this requirement is spelled out in the Act, contrary to the position under the Mental Health Act, which deals only with what the Code of Practice is to cover rather than with the obligation placed upon those for whose guidance it is published. Section 42(5) of the Act goes on to add (again unlike the Mental Health Act where a similar point is in the Code rather than the Act) that:

> *If it appears to a court or tribunal conducting any criminal or civil proceedings that –*
>
> *(a) a provision of (the) Code, or*
>
> *(b) a failure to comply with (the) Code*
>
> *is relevant to a question arising in the proceedings, the provision or failure must be taken into account in deciding the question.*

As the Code itself states, it focuses on those who have a duty of care to someone who lacks the capacity to agree to the care that is being provided. While there is therefore no obligation to comply with the Code, any failure to have regard to any of its guidance must, if considered relevant, be taken into account in deciding whether for example a health or social care professional has acted negligently or failed to comply with good practice. Although spelled out rather than implied, the legal effect is likely to be similar to a failure to follow the Mental Health Act Code of Practice guidance, and the House of Lords' judgment in the *Munjaz* case (2005), which dealt with the status of the Mental Health Act Code of Practice, is likely to apply with equal relevance. The guidance will have to be considered seriously and followed 'unless there are cogent reasons for not doing so' but it will be possible to depart from it without necessarily risking court proceedings; nor will adherence to its guidance determine the issue whether an act, omission to act or decision made in relation to a person lacking capacity constitutes a breach of that person's rights under the European Convention on Human Rights.

ACTIVITY 3.1

Multiple choice questions

Read each question carefully and tick the appropriate box(es). Where a statement is correct, tick the box next to it; if it is incorrect, leave it blank. You may need to tick more than one box per question.

Appendix 5 (pages 145–9) gives the answers.

3.1 The Code of Practice to the Mental Capacity Act 2005 provides guidance for:

    (a) people assessing capacity

    (b) people appointed as attorneys under Lasting Powers of Attorney

    (c) people appointed as guardians under the Mental Health Act 1983

    (d) deputies appointed by the Court of Protection

    (e) Independent Mental Capacity Advocates

    (f) Independent Mental Health Advocates

3.2 Under the Mental Capacity Act a failure to follow the Code of Practice would always lead to court proceedings if reported to the relevant authority:

    (a) True

    (b) False

3.3 Principles for the Mental Capacity Act are set out in the Code of Practice and not in the Act itself:

    (a) True

    (b) False

Chapter 4
Principles (section 1)

Introduction

The Parliamentary Joint Committee which examined the Draft Mental Incapacity Bill was persuaded of the importance of having clear principles explicitly stated in the Act, rather than just in the Code of Practice. One of the most persuasive arguments was that, although lawyers might have been able to identify principles from the provisions of the Act, this was legislation which would be looked at and used by a wide range of people other than lawyers. It was seen as important that people should be aware of these key principles right from the outset.

The popularity of this approach was one of the reasons for a subsequent attempt to have principles inserted at the beginning of the Mental Health Act 1983 when it was reformed in 2007. Chapter 14 examines the links, similarities and differences between the two Acts.

The principles are set out in s 1, right at the beginning of the Act, even before the definition of lack of capacity. There is a strong emphasis within the principles on maximising a person's ability to take part in decision-making. This is reflected throughout the Act and the Code of Practice.

The five principles

As has been noted, these are set out in s 1 of the Act. They are fairly easy to remember and they govern any actions taken within the framework of the Act.

1 The principles

(1) *The following principles apply for the purposes of this Act.*

(2) *A person must be assumed to have capacity unless it is established that he lacks capacity.*

(3) *A person is not to be treated as unable to make a decision unless all practicable steps to help him to do so have been taken without success.*

(4) *A person is not to be treated as unable to make a decision merely because he makes an unwise decision.*

(5) *An act done, or decision made, under this Act for or on behalf of a person who lacks capacity must be done, or made, in his best interests.*

(6) Before the act is done, or the decision is made, regard must be had to whether the purpose for which it is needed can be as effectively achieved in a way that is less restrictive of the person's rights and freedom of action.

Each of the five principles will now be examined to see why it was seen as important to include them on the face of the Act. There will then be some discussion on how each principle should operate in practice. The Code of Practice will be cited where it helps to illustrate how the principles would apply.

A person must be assumed to have capacity

This first principle is consistent with the common law approach which existed before the Act became law. Prior to the introduction of the Mental Capacity Act, if an issue came to court, the burden of proof was on the person alleging a lack of capacity. The standard of proof was 'the balance of probabilities'. This can also be expressed as 'more likely than not'. This standard of proof is repeated in the Mental Capacity Act in s 2 (see Chapter 5) and should not present a problem to those who were used to working in this area within the common law.

Capacity must be considered in relation to a particular decision at a particular time (the 'functional' test). The starting point is then always the presumption of capacity, even if this is very quickly disproved on assessment. For practitioners working with people with severe intellectual disabilities this is sometimes easier said than done. It requires a disciplined mindset to avoid slipping into the practice of assuming incapacity in certain individuals known to the decision-maker, and a need to remind oneself of the fact that a person does not have or lack capacity in general but only in relation to the specific decision which needs to be made at the time.

Fortunately there is no expectation that formal assessments are carried out for every decision. For day-to-day decisions or actions it is sufficient for the person acting to have a reasonable belief that the other person lacks capacity, as long as they have objective reasons for this belief.

Practicable steps to help the person make a decision

This second principle states that:

A person is not to be treated as unable to make a decision unless all practicable steps to help him to do so have been taken without success.

In justifying an intervention a person would need to show that all such practicable steps had been unsuccessful before making a final assessment that the person lacked capacity in relation to the matter in question. It represents a mandatory step to be taken between reaching the provisional conclusion that a person is unable to make a decision and proceeding to determine what is in that person's best interests.

This principle was not expressed as 'all reasonable attempts' (the original expression used by the Law Commission) because critics were concerned that this was too weak and would lead to more people being regarded as incapable than was necessary.

The Code of Practice gives some useful guidance on this issue.

2.7 The kind of support people might need to help them make a decision varies. It depends on personal circumstances, the kind of decision that has to be made and the time available to make the decision. It might include:

- *using a different form of communication (for example, non-verbal communication)*

- *providing information in a more accessible form (for example, photographs, drawings, or tapes)*

- *treating a medical condition which may be affecting the person's capacity or*

- *having a structured programme to improve a person's capacity to make particular decisions (for example, helping a person with learning disabilities to learn new skills).*

The 'time available to make the decision' is of course always a relevant consideration. Chapter 3 of the Code gives more information on ways to help people make decisions for themselves. It includes a number of scenarios which illustrate how staff could provide relevant information, help with specific communication difficulties, put the person at their ease and choose the right time and place to talk to the person concerned.

Many organisations have begun to produce information in different forms to make it more accessible and therefore more likely that people will be able make decisions for themselves.

The introduction to Chapter 3 of the Code also includes the following checklist which is repeated at Appendix 2 in this text.

To help someone make a decision for themselves, check the following points:

Providing relevant information

- *Does the person have all the relevant information they need to make a particular decision?*

- *If they have a choice, have they been given information on all the alternatives?*

Communicating in an appropriate way

- *Could information be explained or presented in a way that is easier for the person to understand (for example, by using simple language or visual aids)?*

- *Have different methods of communication been explored if required, including non-verbal communication?*

- *Could anyone else help with communication (for example, a family member, support worker, interpreter, speech and language therapist or advocate)?*

Making the person feel at ease

- *Are there particular times of day when the person's understanding is better?*

- *Are there particular locations where they may feel more at ease?*

- *Could the decision be put off to see whether the person can make the decision at a later time when circumstances are right for them?*

Supporting the person

- *Can anyone else help or support the person to make choices or express a view?*

Unwise decisions

This third principle states that:

> *A person is not to be treated as unable to make a decision merely because he makes an unwise decision.*

This has been part of the common law since at least as early as 1850 when it was stated in *Bird v Luckie* that, although the law requires a person to be capable of understanding the nature and effect of an action, it does not require that he should behave 'in such a manner as to deserve approbation from the prudent, the wise and the good'.

The Law Commission received an overwhelming majority of opinion that this principle should be explicitly included in the Act. Some concern has been expressed, for example from those giving evidence to the Joint Committee during the pre-legislative scrutiny of the draft Bill, that a decision on its own might just appear unwise but that a series of unwise decisions might actually indicate a lack of capacity. Ashton et al. (2006, p. 68) say that some caution is needed when applying this principle and give some sound advice:

> *Although as a general rule, capacity should be assessed in relation to each particular decision or specific issue, there may be circumstances where a person has an ongoing condition which affects his or her capacity to make a range of interrelated or sequential decisions. One decision on its own may make sense but the combination of decisions may raise doubts as to the person's capacity or at least prompt the need for a proper assessment. But equally, an unwise decision should not, by itself, be sufficient to indicate a lack of capacity.*

Best interests

The fourth principle states that:

> *An act done, or decision made, under this Act for or on behalf of a person who lacks capacity must be done, or made, in his best interests.*

Professionals who have worked with people who lack capacity should be familiar with this principle, as it has been well enshrined within the common law. The significant change introduced by the Mental Capacity Act is the mandatory process whereby best interests should be determined and this is explored further in Chapter 6.

Less restrictive approach

Finally, the fifth principle states that:

> *Before the act is done, or the decision is made, regard must be had to whether the purpose for which it is needed can be as effectively achieved in a way that is less restrictive of the person's rights and freedom of action.*

This is often referred to as the 'least restrictive alternative' approach but this is at slight variance with the wording in the Act itself. One key element in applying this principle is to consider whether the purpose for which the decision is needed 'can be as effectively achieved' in a less restrictive way. There may be less restrictive interventions available but they may not be as effective in achieving the purpose. In applying this principle the question will be asked as to whether any intervention is indeed needed at all.

As with the others, this fifth principle contributes to an overall approach of only making decisions for someone when it is really necessary and of involving them in the process as far as is possible.

ACTIVITY *4.1*

Multiple choice questions
Read each question carefully and tick the appropriate box(es). Where a statement is correct, tick the box next to it; if it is incorrect, leave it blank. You may need to tick more than one box per question.

Appendix 5 (pages 145–9) gives the answers.

4.1 *Key principles of the Mental Capacity Act include:*

(a) *A presumption of capacity exists for all those aged 16 or over* ☐

(b) *All practicable steps are to be taken to help a person make the decision before they're considered incapable* ☐

(c) *An unwise decision implies a lack of capacity* ☐

(d) *Acts done on behalf of an incapacitated person must be in his/her best interests* ☐

(e) *All decisions made on behalf of an incapacitated person must be registered with the Court of Protection* ☐

(f) *Decisions should be the least expensive available in terms of cost to the person* ☐

(g) *Decisions should seek to be less restrictive in terms of the person's rights and freedom of action* ☐

4.2 *The Court of Protection is not covered by the principles as they only apply to other decision-makers under the Act:*

(a) *True* ☐

(b) *False* ☐

Chapter 5

What is lack of capacity? (sections 2–3)

Introduction

One of the benefits of having an Act of Parliament in this complex area is that, at last, we have a single definition of what amounts to a lack of capacity.

Section 2 of the Act states that:

> a person lacks capacity in relation to a matter if at the material time he is unable to make a decision for himself in relation to the matter because of an impairment of, or a disturbance in the functioning of, the mind or brain.

It does not matter if this impairment or disturbance is permanent or temporary and some decisions will need to be made even though a person may regain capacity within a short space of time.

The standard of proof is outlined in s 2(4).

> In proceedings under this Act or any other enactment, any question whether a person lacks capacity within the meaning of this Act must be decided on the balance of probabilities.

If the diagnostic test makes the Act applicable to an individual, s 3 then provides the test for incapacity that should be used. It is an interesting development from tests that had been established by the courts, such as in the case of C *(Adult: Refusal of Medical Treatment)* 1994. The section 3 test is that:

> a person is unable to make a decision for himself if he is unable –
>
> (a) to understand the information relevant to the decision,
>
> (b) to retain that information,
>
> (c) to use or weigh that information as part of the process of making the decision, or
>
> (d) to communicate his decision (whether by talking, using sign language or any other means).

An inability to satisfy any one of these four conditions would render the person incapable.

A functional approach

This approach of defining a person as incapacitated only in relation to a particular decision at a particular time has been described as the functional approach. This contrasts with an approach that states that because a person has a particular medical condition they lack capacity generally.

There is in effect a two-staged approach to determining lack of capacity. First it needs to be established that the person has an impairment or a disturbance in the functioning of the mind or brain. Secondly, it then needs to be established that this is sufficient to prevent the person from being able to make the decision in question at a particular time.

The phrase 'a disturbance in the functioning of, the mind or brain' effectively includes many people who would fall outside of the definition of mental disorder for the purposes of the Mental Health Act 1983. A person might present with short-term effects of alcohol or drug use or the effects of a physical disorder which renders the person temporarily incapacitated in terms of making a number of decisions. Despite the changes in s 1 of the Mental Health Act 1983 (which are expected to take effect in 2008) this distinction will continue.

In addition, a person may well have a mental disorder but still be capable of making a particular decision. They could even be detained under the Mental Health Act but the relevant decision happens to fall outside the scope of that Act (e.g. treatment for a physical disorder or a social decision).

Non-discrimination

Both in this part of the Act, and in relation to determining best interests, a principle of 'equal consideration' applies.

Section 2(3) states:

> *A lack of capacity cannot be established merely by reference to –*
>
> *(a) a person's age or appearance, or*
>
> *(b) a condition of his, or an aspect of his behaviour, which might lead others to make unjustified assumptions about his capacity.*

This was an amendment proposed by the Making Decisions Alliance which was an organisation made up from a number of charities who were campaigning for the Act. The Alliance was concerned that prejudice against certain groups would disadvantage them. Rather than becoming one of the five key principles this was included in the part of the Act defining lack of capacity and in the process of establishing best interests. The words 'appearance' and 'condition' would cover a wide range of situations such as visible disability, skin colour, dress, and mental disorder.

The section 3 test

The four elements of the test will now be considered:

(a) Understanding the information relevant to the decision

Chapter 4 of the Code of Practice identifies that relevant information would need to include the nature of the decision, the reason why the decision is needed, and the likely effects of deciding one way or another or of making no decision at all.

Section 3(4) of the Act states that:

> The information relevant to a decision includes information about the reasonably foreseeable consequences of –
>
> (a) deciding one way or another, or
>
> (b) failing to make the decision.

Section 3(2) states that:

> A person is not to be regarded as unable to understand the information relevant to a decision if he is able to understand an explanation of it given to him in a way that is appropriate to his circumstances (using simple language, visual aids or any other means).

The Code of Practice gives a range of examples of how people might be helped to understand the information by presenting it in different ways, such as with sign language, visual representations or computer support.

(b) Retaining the relevant information

Section 3(3) states that:

> The fact that a person is able to retain the information relevant to a decision for a short period only does not prevent him from being regarded as able to make the decision.

Essentially the person would need to retain the information long enough to reach the end of the process of decision-making, including communicating the decision. For more straightforward decisions this may just require a matter of a few minutes but for more complex decisions there might be a risk that the person would forget some of the information before they had finalised and communicated their decision. The Code of Practice (at para 4.20) suggests that notebooks, photographs, posters, videos and voice recorders may help someone to record and retain information.

(c) Using or weighing the relevant information as part of the process of making the decision

This is based on the existing common law position that has been established through a series of cases. The Code of Practice gives two examples at para 4.22.

> A person with the eating disorder anorexia nervosa may understand information about the consequences of not eating. But their compulsion not to eat might be too strong for them to ignore. Some people who have serious brain damage might make impulsive decisions regardless of information they have been given or their understanding of it.

(d) Communicating the decision (whether by talking, using sign language or any other means)

It will be unusual that a person would be unable to communicate if they have successfully completed the first three parts of the capacity test. However there is a rare condition known as 'locked-in syndrome' where a person may be conscious but unable to speak or move in such a way as to be able to communicate. Clearly all practicable steps should be taken to help someone to communicate. This might involve speech or language therapists. Note that the section refers to an *inability* to communicate the decision, not a *refusal* or *reluctance* to do so.

Situations requiring the capacity test

When someone suspects that a person may lack capacity to make a particular decision, and where they consider that a decision needs to be made, that person will usually be the person applying the test. For many decisions that will be an informal carer. They do not need to be experts in assessing capacity but they do need to have reasonable grounds for believing that the person lacks capacity if they intend to intervene. There would need to be objective grounds for their opinion. The Code's checklist (set out in this book on page 27 and also at Appendix 2) may be helpful as part of this process.

For a legal transaction a solicitor (or other legal practitioner) must assess a person's ability to instruct them. The information that will need to be understood will vary according to the transaction but the test itself will be as outlined in this chapter. Where there is doubt about the effect of any impairment, expert advice should be sought.

Whenever professional opinion is sought it should be remembered that the final decision about a person's capacity rests with the person making the decision in question. The Court of Protection would be the final decision-maker in disputed cases.

For healthcare decisions the Code of Practice notes at para 4.40 that:

> If a doctor or healthcare professional proposes treatment or an examination, they must assess the person's capacity to consent. In settings such as a hospital, this can involve the multi-disciplinary team (a team of people from different professional backgrounds who share responsibility for a patient). But ultimately, it is up to the professional responsible for the person's treatment to make sure that capacity has been assessed.

What is a reasonable belief that someone lacks capacity?

When someone suspects that a person may lack capacity to make a particular decision how far do they need to go in testing this? We noted in Chapter 4 that for day-to-day decisions or actions it is sufficient for the person acting to have a 'reasonable belief' that the other person lacks capacity. Carers do not have to be experts in assessing capacity. But to have protection from liability when providing care or treatment they must have this 'reasonable belief' that the other person lacks capacity to make relevant decisions about their care or treatment. This is acceptable as long as they have objective reasons for this belief.

The decision-maker must have taken reasonable steps to establish that the other person lacks capacity to make a decision or to consent to an act at the time the decision or consent is needed. They must also establish that the act or decision is in the person's best interests.

They do not usually need to follow formal processes or involve a professional to make an assessment. However, if somebody challenges their assessment they must be able to describe the steps they have taken.

Paragraph 4.45 of the Code of Practice notes that:

> *Professionals, who are qualified in their particular field, are normally expected to undertake a fuller assessment, reflecting their higher degree of knowledge and experience, than family members or other carers who have no formal qualifications.*

The same paragraph sets out a helpful list of pointers to consider. A more formal checklist follows but this is a useful summary of some key points.

- *Start by assuming the person has capacity to make the specific decision. Is there anything to prove otherwise?*

- *Does the person have a previous diagnosis of disability or mental disorder? Does that condition now affect their capacity to make this decision? If there has been no previous diagnosis, it may be best to get a medical opinion.*

- *Make every effort to communicate with the person to explain what is happening.*

- *Make every effort to try to help the person make the decision in question.*

- *See if there is a way to explain or present information about the decision in a way that makes it easier to understand. If the person has a choice, do they have information about all the options?*

- *Can the decision be delayed to take time to help the person make the decision, or to give the person time to regain the capacity to make the decision for themselves?*

- *Does the person understand what decision they need to make and why they need to make it?*

- *Can they understand information about the decision? Can they retain it, use it and weigh it to make the decision?*

- *Be aware that the fact that a person agrees with you or assents to what is proposed does not necessarily mean that they have capacity to make the decision.*

A checklist for assessing capacity

The quick summary at the beginning of Chapter 4 of the Code of Practice provides a useful checklist for assessing capacity. This list is repeated in this book at Appendix 3.

Assessing capacity

This checklist is a summary of points to consider when assessing a person's capacity to make a specific decision:

Presuming someone has capacity
- The starting assumption must always be that a person has the capacity to make a decision, unless it can be established that they lack capacity.

Understanding what is meant by capacity and lack of capacity
- A person's capacity must be assessed specifically in terms of their capacity to make a particular decision at the time it needs to be made.

Treating everyone equally
- A person's capacity must not be judged simply on the basis of their age, appearance, condition or an aspect of their behaviour.

Supporting the person to make the decision for themselves
- It is important to take all possible steps to try to help people make a decision for themselves . . .

Assessing capacity
- Anyone assessing someone's capacity to make a decision for themselves should use the two-stage test of capacity.

- Does the person have an impairment of the mind or brain, or is there some sort of disturbance affecting the way their brain or mind works? (It doesn't matter whether the impairment or disturbance is temporary or permanent.)

- If so, does that impairment or disturbance mean that the person is unable to make the decision in question at the time it needs to be made?

Assessing ability to make a decision
- Does the person have a general understanding of what decision they need to make and why they need to make it?

- Does the person have a general understanding of the likely consequences of making, or not making, this decision?

- Is the person able to understand, retain, use and weigh up the information relevant to this decision?

- Can the person communicate their decision (by talking, using sign language or any other means)? Would the services of a professional (such as a speech and language therapist) be helpful?

Assessing capacity to make more complex or serious decisions
- Is there a need for a more thorough assessment (perhaps by involving a doctor or other professional expert)?

Recording by professionals

Where a professional has carried out an assessment of a person's capacity to make a particular decision this should be recorded in the relevant professional records. Doctors and healthcare professionals would be expected to record this in the patient's clinical notes. Solicitors should keep records on their clients' files when they have assessed capacity to give instructions or carry out a legal transaction. Social care staff will keep records according to their area of work (e.g. within the Care Programme Approach or relevant assessment process) and records will need to be quickly accessible if they are to be helpful.

ACTIVITY **5.1**

Multiple choice questions

Read each question carefully and tick the appropriate box(es). Where a statement is correct, tick the box next to it; if it is incorrect, leave it blank. You may need to tick more than one box per question.

Appendix 5 (pages 145–9) gives the answers.

5.1 *A decision on a person's mental capacity needs to be made in relation to the particular matter at the time when the decision has to be made:*

(a) *True* ☐

(b) *False* ☐

5.2 *The test for capacity under the Mental Capacity Act is whether the person can:*

(a) *Understand the relevant information* ☐

(b) *Retain the relevant information* ☐

(c) *Believe the relevant information* ☐

(d) *Use or weigh the relevant information as part of the decision-making process* ☐

(e) *Communicate the decision* ☐

(f) *Read and sign a consent form* ☐

5.3 *The fact that a person is able to retain the information relevant to a decision for a short period only will prevent him from being regarded as able to make the decision:*

(a) *True* ☐

(b) *False* ☐

Chapter 6
Best interests (section 4)

Introduction

Many professionals will be familiar with the principle of acting in the best interests of a person who lacks capacity. This has long been established within the common law and more recently the principle has been extended by case law to go beyond just medical decisions to include social welfare matters.

What people will need to become familiar with, though, is the Act's new requirement that certain steps will need to be followed in determining what would be in a person's best interests.

The checklist approach

The approach adopted by the Mental Capacity Act is to set out a checklist of common factors which as a minimum should be considered on each occasion that a decision needs to be made. The Law Commission (1995, para 3.28) was aware that care should be taken not to make this approach too unwieldy when it stated:

> First, a checklist must not unduly burden any decision-maker or encourage unnecessary intervention; secondly it must not be applied too rigidly and should leave room for all considerations relevant to the particular case; thirdly, it should be confined to major points, so that it can adapt to changing views and attitudes.

The principle of equal consideration

As with the definition of mental incapacity, the best interests checklist starts with this anti-discriminatory principle. Section 4(1) states:

> In determining for the purposes of this Act what is in a person's best interests, the person making the determination must not make it merely on the basis of –
>
> (a) the person's age or appearance, or
>
> (b) a condition of his, or an aspect of his behaviour, which might lead others to make unjustified assumptions about what might be in his best interests.

In practice this means, for example, that decisions about best interests should not be made on pre-conceived ideas about the quality of life of older people or people with severe disabilities. One would hope that this would not be the case but the Act covers such a wide range of people and circumstances that it was considered necessary to include such a phrase.

All relevant circumstances

This is a catch-all expression which means that, as well as following the rest of the list, a person should consider all other relevant matters which affect the particular decision that is under consideration.

Subsection 11 defines 'relevant circumstances' as those:

(a) *of which the person making the determination is aware, and*

(b) *which it would be reasonable to regard as relevant.*

This allows for a degree of flexibility so that one would not have to make exhaustive enquiries in every set of circumstances.

Regaining capacity

This was added to the original list proposed by the Law Commission.

Section 4(3) requires a decision-maker to consider:

(a) *whether it is likely that the person will at some time have capacity in relation to the matter in question, and*

(b) *if it appears likely that he will, when that is likely to be.*

If it is possible to put off the decision until the person can make it for themselves, then this is what should happen. In an emergency this may not be possible. It may, however, be feasible to limit the scope of a decision so that a small intervention can be followed by the person making more significant decisions when they have regained capacity.

The Code of Practice (para 5.28) includes a list of indicators that a person might regain or develop capacity in the future:

- *the cause of the lack of capacity can be treated, either by medication or some other form of treatment or therapy*

- *the lack of capacity is likely to decrease in time (for example, where it is caused by the effects of medication or alcohol, or following a sudden shock)*

- *a person with learning disabilities may learn new skills or be subject to new experiences which increase their understanding and ability to make certain decisions*

- *the person may have a condition which causes capacity to come and go at various times (such as some forms of mental illness) so it may be possible to arrange for the decision to be made during a time when they do have capacity*

- *a person previously unable to communicate may learn a new form of communication.*

Participation of the individual

Section 4(4) requires the decision-maker, as far as is reasonably practicable,

to permit and encourage the person to participate, or to improve his ability to participate, as fully as possible in any act done for him and any decision affecting him.

The 'practicable steps' to help the person make the decision may not have been successful but they will still be relevant for this part of the checklist. Even if the person is unable to make the decision their maximum involvement in the process should be encouraged and facilitated. As well as helping to determine what is in the person's best interests this process may gradually move the person towards a greater ability to make related or simpler decisions.

Life-sustaining treatment

Much of the debate in Parliament before the Act was passed was focused on life and death issues involving people who lacked capacity. There was some concern that the Act would lead to the introduction of euthanasia or assisted suicide. An amendment was introduced in the House of Lords. The final wording is contained in s 4(5):

Where the determination relates to life-sustaining treatment he must not, in considering whether the treatment is in the best interests of the person concerned, be motivated by a desire to bring about his death.

As long as the motivation is not to bring about a person's death it will still be possible to withdraw life-sustaining treatment in the final stages of a terminal illness or for someone in a persistent vegetative state if there was no prospect of recovery. The best interests of the person might lead to this conclusion.

Similarly a drug such as diamorphine might be known to be likely to hasten someone's death, but it may be given for pain relief if that is the motivation rather than to bring about their early death.

Paragraph 5.31 of the Code of Practice approaches the issue in this way:

All reasonable steps which are in the person's best interests should be taken to prolong their life. There will be a limited number of cases where treatment is futile, overly burdensome to the patient or where there is no prospect of recovery. In circumstances such as these, it may be that an assessment of best interests leads to the conclusion that it would be in the best interests of the patient to withdraw or withhold life-sustaining treatment, even if this may result in the person's death. The decision-maker must make a decision based on the best interests of the person who lacks capacity. They must not be motivated by a desire to bring about the person's death for whatever reason, even if this is from a sense of compassion. Healthcare and social care staff should also refer to relevant professional guidance when making decisions regarding life-sustaining treatment.

Wishes, feelings, beliefs and values

Section 4(6) requires the decision-maker, 'so far as is reasonably ascertainable', to consider:

(a) *the person's past and present wishes and feelings (and, in particular, any relevant written statement made by him when he had capacity),*

(b) *the beliefs and values that would be likely to influence his decision if he had capacity, and*

(c) *the other factors that he would be likely to consider if he were able to do so.*

This requires the decision-maker to concentrate on the person in question and to make efforts to find out about any views they may have expressed in the past, including any written statements. Formal advance decisions in the Act only cover advance refusals of medical treatment (which may include psychiatric treatment subject to the limitations noted elsewhere when Part 4 of the Mental Health Act is relevant). However, this part of the Act may encourage some people to record their views, knowing that they will need to be taken into account by anyone determining their best interests at a later date in the event of their losing capacity.

Such recorded views would not be binding on later decision-makers, because they might then conflict with what is in the person's best interests. However, recording views would make them more accessible to decision-makers at a later date and a number of people may well choose to make such advance statements, knowing that they would not be binding. It is also worth noting that a person could specify people that they would like to be consulted in future on particular matters.

The Code of Practice (para 5.46) notes that a person's beliefs and values might be deduced from things such as their cultural background, religious beliefs, political convictions or past behaviour or habits.

The views of other people

This consideration includes an important change in the law. This is the first time that carers, family members and others have had a statutory right to be consulted on decisions affecting a mentally incapacitated person. People used to be asked what they knew of the person's own wishes but did not have the right to state what they thought should happen themselves.

Section 4(7) requires the decision-maker to take into account, if it is practicable and appropriate to consult them, the views of:

(a) *anyone named by the person as someone to be consulted on the matter in question or on matters of that kind,*

(b) *anyone engaged in caring for the person or interested in his welfare,*

(c) *any donee of a lasting power of attorney granted by the person, and*

(d) any deputy appointed for the person by the court,

as to what would be in the person's best interests and, in particular, as to the matters mentioned in subsection (6).

This would not then bind the decision-maker to follow what others have said, but they must give their views due consideration. Those caring for the person could involve children as there is no age limit set by this provision. The potential overlap with the role of the nearest relative under the Mental Health Act is explored in Chapter 16.

If the decision-maker decides that it is not practical or appropriate to consult someone on this list the Code suggests (5.51) that they should be able to explain why this was the case and that it would be good practice to record these reasons.

Best interests checklist

These key steps are from the quick summary in Chapter 5 of the Code of Practice. They are reproduced at Appendix 4 as a quick guide.

A person trying to work out the best interests of a person who lacks capacity to make a particular decision ('lacks capacity') should:

Encourage participation
- do whatever is possible to permit and encourage the person to take part, or to improve their ability to take part, in making the decision

Identify all relevant circumstances
- try to identify all the things that the person who lacks capacity would take into account if they were making the decision or acting for themselves

Find out the person's views
- try to find out the views of the person who lacks capacity, including:

  - the person's past and present wishes and feelings – these may have been expressed verbally, in writing or through behaviour or habits

  - any beliefs and values (e.g. religious, cultural, moral or political) that would be likely to influence the decision in question

  - any other factors the person themselves would be likely to consider if they were making the decision or acting for themselves.

Avoid discrimination
- not make assumptions about someone's best interests simply on the basis of the person's age, appearance, condition or behaviour.

Assess whether the person might regain capacity
- consider whether the person is likely to regain capacity (e.g. after receiving medical treatment). If so, can the decision wait until then?

If the decision concerns life-sustaining treatment

- not be motivated in any way by a desire to bring about the person's death. They should not make assumptions about the person's quality of life.

Consult others

- if it is practical and appropriate to do so, consult other people for their views about the person's best interests and to see if they have any information about the person's wishes and feelings, beliefs and values. In particular, try to consult:

  - anyone previously named by the person as someone to be consulted on either the decision in question or on similar issues

  - anyone engaged in caring for the person

  - close relatives, friends or others who take an interest in the person's welfare

  - any attorney appointed under a Lasting Power of Attorney or Enduring Power of Attorney made by the person

  - any deputy appointed by the Court of Protection to make decisions for the person.

- For decisions about major medical treatment or where the person should live and where there is no-one who fits into any of the above categories, an Independent Mental Capacity Advocate (IMCA) must be consulted (see Code, Chapter 10 for more information about IMCAs).

- When consulting, remember that the person who lacks the capacity to make the decision or act for themselves still has a right to keep their affairs private – so it would not be right to share every piece of information with everyone.

Avoid restricting the person's rights

- see if there are other options that may be less restrictive of the person's rights.

Take all of this into account

- weigh up all of these factors in order to work out what is in the person's best interests.

ACTIVITY **6.1**

Multiple choice questions

Read each question carefully and tick the appropriate box(es). Where a statement is correct, tick the box next to it; if it is incorrect, leave it blank. You may need to tick more than one box per question.

Appendix 5 (pages 145–9) gives the answers.

6.1 According to the Mental Capacity Act decisions made in relation to an incapacitated person must be in that person's best interests but the list of points to consider are in the Code rather than being set out in the statute:

(a) True ☐

(b) False ☐

6.2 Following best interests could lead to the withdrawal of life-sustaining treatment:

(a) True ☐

(b) False ☐

6.3 The best interests checklist includes:

(a) Decisions should not be based on a person's appearance ☐

(b) Waiting where possible for the person to regain capacity ☐

(c) Never going against the incapacitated person's current views ☐

(d) Consulting anyone who has been named by the person ☐

(e) Seeking to incur minimal expense for the person themselves ☐

(f) Identifying all relevant circumstances ☐

Chapter 7

Protection for those making decisions (sections 5 to 8)

Introduction

Many professionals are understandably concerned about their legal liability if they intervene and make decisions for someone which turn out later to have negative consequences. The Mental Capacity Act approaches this issue in an interesting way. Essentially, if it can be demonstrated that the requirements of the Act have been followed by the decision-maker (D) it will be as if the person who lacked capacity (P) had made the decision themselves.

Section 5 acts

Section 5 is worded as follows:

> *(1) If a person ('D') does an act in connection with the care or treatment of another person ('P'), the act is one to which this section applies if –*
>
> *(a) before doing the act, D takes reasonable steps to establish whether P lacks capacity in relation to the matter in question, and*
>
> *(b) when doing the act, D reasonably believes –*
>
> *(i) that P lacks capacity in relation to the matter, and*
>
> *(ii) that it will be in P's best interests for the act to be done.*
>
> *(2) D does not incur any liability in relation to the act that he would not have incurred if P –*
>
> *(a) had had capacity to consent in relation to the matter, and*
>
> *(b) had consented to D's doing the act.*

So the key for the decision-maker is to clearly identify the act and why it needs to be performed, and then that they have a reasonable belief:

- that the person lacks capacity in relation to the matter at the particular time of intervention, and

- that it will be in the person's best interests.

Chapters 5 and 6 should equip people with the knowledge required for these two stages. If the person making the decision can confirm that he has applied these tests appropriately he will be safe from legal liability. Note that in most cases it will not be possible for someone to demonstrate that he has acted in the best interests of an incapacitated person without having applied the section 4 checklist. No checklist, no best interests, so no section 5 protection.

Four further comments are necessary at this stage.

Firstly, s 5 does not mean that staff can act recklessly or negligently.

Section 5(3) states:

> *(3) Nothing in this section excludes a person's civil liability for loss or damage, or his criminal liability, resulting from his negligence in doing the act.*

The second point is that s 5 does not allow a decision-maker to override a valid and applicable advance refusal of treatment.

The third comment concerns LPAs and deputies. Section 6(6) states:

> *Section 5 does not authorise a person to do an act which conflicts with a decision made, within the scope of his authority and in accordance with this Part, by –*
>
> *(a) a donee of a lasting power of attorney granted by P, or*
>
> *(b) a deputy appointed for P by the court.*

There will be more of an onus on people to check in certain situations as to whether there is an LPA or whether a deputy has been appointed. In cases of doubt the Office of the Public Guardian will help with this. If a person makes a decision in genuine ignorance of such a person existing or having made a conflicting decision they will be covered by s 5.

If there is any uncertainty over these last two points and where a person's life may be at risk, s 6(7) states:

> *But nothing in subsection (6) stops a person –*
>
> *(a) providing life-sustaining treatment, or*
>
> *(b) doing any act which he reasonably believes to be necessary to prevent a serious deterioration in P's condition,*
>
> *while a decision as respects any relevant issue is sought from the court.*

The final issue concerns restraint. If restraint is used, s 6 makes further conditions before people can rely on the protection of s 5.

Restraint

The use of restraint is controversial. It may well be that, in the past, under the common law, restraint has not been used when it would have been appropriate because the staff concerned were not sure of their legal position. There have also been a number of occasions when people have justified the use of restraint by saying it was necessary in a person's best interests when closer examination suggested that this was not the case. The hope is that the clarification of this area in the Act will lead to more consistent and positive practice.

Restraint is defined as:

(i) *the use or threat of force in any action which the person resists, or*

(ii) *any restriction of a person's liberty of movement, whether or not they resist.*

If restraint amounts to deprivation of liberty this goes beyond the scope of s 5. This issue will be explored in more depth under a separate heading below. The actual wording in s 6(5) is:

D does more than merely restrain P if he deprives P of his liberty within the meaning of Article 5(1) of the Human Rights Convention (whether or not D is a public authority).

For the person using restraint to keep the protection of s 5 there are two conditions. The position is expressed in s 6 in the following way:

(1) *If D does an act that is intended to restrain P, it is not an act to which s 5 applies unless two further conditions are satisfied.*

(2) *The first condition is that D reasonably believes that it is necessary to do the act in order to prevent harm to P.*

(3) *The second is that the act is a proportionate response to –*

(a) *the likelihood of P's suffering harm, and*

(b) *the seriousness of that harm.*

It is not enough to argue that restraint is necessary to prevent the person from harming someone else. Intervention in these circumstances may well be appropriate but it would not link with the protection of s 5 and would be justified, if at all, under common law. For restraint to be justified under the Mental Capacity Act there needs to be a sufficient likelihood of the person suffering harm and the potential harm needs to be serious enough to make this a proportionate response.

Deprivation of liberty

We noted above that a decision-maker does more than merely restrain a person if he deprives him of his liberty within the meaning of Article 5(1) of the Human Rights Convention (whether or not the decision-maker is a public authority). Article 5 states:

No one shall be deprived of their liberty except for specific cases and in accordance with procedure prescribed by law e.g. after conviction, lawful arrest on suspicion of having committed an offence, lawful detention of person of unsound mind, to prevent spread of infectious diseases. Everyone deprived of liberty by arrest or detention shall be entitled to take proceedings by which the lawfulness of the detention shall be decided speedily by a Court and release ordered if the detention is not lawful.

The Mental Health Act 1983 has a procedure to detain mentally disordered persons. In certain circumstances this would be an appropriate response where interventions under the Mental Capacity Act were involving restraint which was beginning to approach a deprivation of liberty. There is more information in Chapter 15 about links between these two Acts.

Where a person lacks the capacity to decide about being in a particular place, and is in effect deprived of their liberty there are several options:

(i) scale down the level of restrictions (including any restraint) to what would be seen as a restriction of movement rather than a deprivation of liberty;

(ii) arrange an assessment under the Mental Health Act with a view to using its powers;

(iii) make an application to the Court of Protection to make a personal welfare decision;

(iv) follow the new 'Bournewood' procedures (not yet in force at the time of writing) as covered in Chapter 16;

(v) consider short-term or emergency use of common law powers.

What amounts to deprivation of liberty?

This is a question that has troubled mental health professionals, especially since the *Bournewood* case which is examined in more detail in Chapter 15. There is no single factor which determines deprivation of liberty. In *Bournewood* (*HL v UK*, 2004) the European Court of Human Rights stated that the difference was one of degree or intensity rather than nature or substance. It may depend on the type of care being provided, how long the situation lasts, what the effects are and how the situation came about. There is some guidance in the Code of Practice (para 6.52) as to what factors contribute to deprivation of liberty. These have been drawn from European case law.

The European Court of Human Rights has identified the following as factors contributing to deprivation of liberty in its judgments on cases to date:

- *restraint was used, including sedation, to admit a person who is resisting*

- *professionals exercised complete and effective control over care and movement for a significant period*

- *professionals exercised control over assessments, treatment, contacts and residence*

- *the person would be prevented from leaving if they made a meaningful attempt to do so*

- *a request by carers for the person to be discharged to their care was refused*

- *the person was unable to maintain social contacts because of restrictions placed on access to other people*

- *the person lost autonomy because they were under continuous supervision and control.*

Chapter 15 looks at the current overlaps with mental health law in this area and Chapter 16 sets out the Government's attempt to fill the 'Bournewood Gap'. These amendments to the Mental Capacity Act are not expected to be in force until at least April 2009 so they are contained in a separate chapter.

Financial implications of section 5 decisions

Another area of concern for those making decisions on someone else's behalf is where the money will come from if there are any financial implications of the decision. Paying for goods and services provided is covered by s 7 which states that:

> *(1) If necessary goods or services are supplied to a person who lacks capacity to contract for the supply, he must pay a reasonable price for them.*

> *(2) 'Necessary' means suitable to a person's condition in life and to his actual requirements at the time when the goods or services are supplied.*

If a decision-maker is involved with an act which involves expenditure s 8(1) allows them:

> *(a) to pledge P's credit for the purpose of the expenditure, and*

> *(b) to apply money in P's possession for meeting the expenditure.*

Similarly, if the expenditure is borne for P by D, it is lawful for D to reimburse himself out of money in P's possession, or to be otherwise indemnified by P.

Key checks for decision-makers

1. What is the act or decision?

2. Why does it need to be performed now?

3. Do you have a reasonable belief that the person lacks capacity in relation to the matter at the particular time of intervention?

4. Can you confirm that it will be in the person's best interests and that you have followed the checklist?

Chapter 8
Lasting Powers of Attorney (sections 9–14 and 22–23)

General

Since the Enduring Powers of Attorney Act 1985 it has been possible to create a Power of Attorney which 'endures' beyond the time when the donor loses mental capacity. However, this has been limited to decisions and acts concerning the donor's property and affairs. It has not been possible to include personal welfare matters (including consenting to medical treatment) within an Enduring Power of Attorney (EPA). This was in line with the general principle of common law that no one can consent on behalf of another adult to a medical procedure. Hospital consent forms have sometimes been signed by a relative of, for example, an adult with learning difficulties unable to consent for him or herself, without people realising that this does not provide a valid consent in law. Even if the High Court has been approached regarding an issue surrounding the giving or withdrawal of treatment to or from someone who lacks capacity it might grant a declaration that it would be lawful to proceed or not as the case may be, but the court would not consent on behalf of the patient concerned. Thus introducing substituted decision-making in the field of personal welfare, health care and consent to medical treatment is one of the more controversial innovations of the Mental Capacity Act, not least because of the additional opportunities for abuse that might be presented. Even if the relationship at the time of creation of the Lasting Power of Attorney was one of unqualified trust, that is no guarantee of the position at some time in the future. The term 'donee' used here equates to the attorney.

What is a Lasting Power of Attorney?

A Lasting Power of Attorney is defined in s 9(1) as:

a power of attorney under which the donor ('P') confers on the donee (or donees) authority to make decisions about all or any of the following –

(a) P's personal welfare or specified matters concerning P's personal welfare, and

(b) P's property and affairs or specified matters concerning P's property and affairs,

and which includes authority to make such decisions in circumstances where P no longer has capacity.

Section 64(2) states that references in the Act to making decisions in relation to LPAs include, where appropriate, acting on decisions made.

From 1 October 2007 no new EPAs can be made. They are replaced by Lasting Powers of Attorney (LPAs) which may be either a property and affairs LPA or a personal welfare LPA. If a person wishes to cover both areas of decision-making then separate LPAs are required.

What can an LPA cover?

The list of actions and decisions which a property and affairs LPA might cover is not set out in the Act; however at 7.36 of the Code of Practice numerous examples are given including:

- buying or selling property

- operating bank accounts

- dealing with tax affairs

- paying outgoings

- investing savings

- making gifts

- applying for entitlement to NHS or social care entitlement

- claiming, receiving and using benefits.

Similarly the scope of a personal welfare LPA is not set out in the Act (although s 11(7)(c) provides that it may include giving or refusing consent to medical treatment) but is illustrated in the Code of Practice at 7.21. It could include

- decisions about where the donor should live

- who may have contact with him

- day-to-day care

- rights of access to personal information about the donor

- whether the donor should take part in social activities, leisure activities, education or training.

Section 11(8) states that where the personal welfare LPA includes refusal of or consent to medical treatment, this will not include life-sustaining treatment (as defined in s 4(10)) unless expressly stated in the LPA.

The formal requirements

Because of the increased opportunities for abuse there has been a corresponding increase in the safeguards which the Government felt it necessary to introduce to give donors additional protections. One such safeguard is the very much more detailed and complex formal requirements needed both to make and register LPAs. These formal requirements are set out in s 10 and in Schedule 1 to the Act, but more particularly in the Lasting Powers of Attorney, Enduring Powers of Attorney and Public Guardian Regulations (2007, No. 1253).

While it is understandable that increased formality might be required in respect of the novel introduction of substituted decision-making for personal welfare and medical matters it is less obvious why this should be so for a property and affairs LPA covering similar ground to an EPA. So the forms required for each run to 25 pages and include detailed prescribed information. The prescribed information includes

- the s 1 principles;
- guidance about choosing an attorney or a replacement;
- when the attorney can act;
- what decisions the attorney can make;
- the restrictions that can be imposed;
- paying the attorney;
- registering the LPA;
- in the case of a personal welfare LPA, the special requirements relating to life-sustaining treatment.

In the LPA the donor can name up to five people who must be notified when an application to register is made. In addition an independent person has to certify that in his or her opinion the donor is making the LPA of his or her own free will and that he or she understands its purpose and the powers being given to the attorney. Should the donor decide not to name any people who must be first notified there must then be a second independent person providing an additional certificate.

The LPA cannot be used until it has been registered by the Office of Public Guardian (which controls and maintains the register of LPAs) and stamped on every page. It will be interesting to see whether the enhanced safeguards provide incentives to donors to make LPAs or whether they will be put off by the degree of formality, complexity and expense that will be involved.

For the most part the Mental Capacity Act applies to those aged over 16. However, for an LPA both the donor and the attorney must be over 18 and have capacity to execute or operate it respectively. Property and affairs attorneys may not be undischarged bankrupts.

To what controls are attorneys and LPAs subject?

All attorneys are subject to the s 1 principles and the best interests 'checklist' of s 4. In addition s 42(4) requires an attorney to have regard to the Code of Practice. So for example an attorney will have to

- assume capacity on the part of a donor;

- take all practical steps to help him to make the decision for himself;

- consult as required by s 4;

- so far as is reasonably ascertainable consider the donor's past and present wishes, beliefs and values.

The attorney is also by s 11 subject to similar limitations on the use of restraint imposed generally by s 6 and cannot use restraint or restrictions of movement which amount to a deprivation of liberty within the meaning of Article 5 of the European Convention on Human Rights. Appointing an attorney does not therefore alter the requirements for assessing capacity or determining best interests, nor does it displace the s 1 principles. What the donor is doing is identifying the person who will make the decisions, not changing the requirements of the Act as to how those decisions should be reached.

How might an LPA be limited in scope?

An LPA, whether personal welfare or property and affairs, does not have to cover all possible areas of decision-making. The donor could limit it to financial issues only or to certain types of medical treatment, or to the issue of where the donor is to live. Or the donor could grant a general power but exclude one single area of decision-making such as, for example, who may be allowed to have contact with the donor. Section 9(4)(b) states that the authority conferred by an LPA is subject to any conditions or restrictions specified in it. These could include a requirement that the attorney first consult with a named person before reaching his decision or with different named persons in respect of different areas of decision-making. An attorney could approach the Court of Protection for authority under s 23(2)(b) to make a decision which does not fall within the ambit of the LPA. An example would be where the attorney wishes to make a gift to a relative of the donor other than on a 'customary occasion' permitted by s 12(2).

Several attorneys may be appointed by the donor under an LPA. The donor may wish to appoint different people to deal with his property and affairs from those he wishes to make personal welfare decisions for him. Where more than one person is appointed the LPA must specify whether they are to act jointly or jointly and severally. If jointly then all appointed must agree before the decision can be effective, if jointly and severally then any of the attorneys will have the authority individually. If the LPA fails to specify whether the attorneys are to act jointly or jointly and severally, it will be assumed that they are to act jointly (s 10(5)). The donor may in the LPA identify a substitute attorney should the original attorney die, become incapacitated, bankrupt or disclaim his appointment, or should the donor's marriage be dissolved. However the attorney himself has no such power to appoint a substitute or successor.

A personal welfare LPA can only be effective once the donor has become, or the attorney believes he has become, incapacitated. This contrasts with the situation under an EPA or a property and affairs LPA which may, if the LPA so provides, take effect before the donor loses capacity.

In keeping with the Act's requirement that the question of capacity is decision-specific, in the case of a personal welfare LPA, or a property and affairs LPA which provides that it is only effective once the donor has lost capacity, the attorney will only be able to make those decisions for which the donor lacks capacity at the time. As mentioned above an attorney must take all practical steps to enable the donor to continue to make decisions in those areas where he retains capacity, limiting his involvement as decision-maker to those where the donor is incapable of making the decision for himself. He will have to have regard to the definition of incapacity and the test of incapacity set out in ss 2 and 3. This could lead to problems in practice where the attorney and health or social care professional have different views as to the person's capacity to make the decision in question. Chapter 15 of the Code of Practice gives guidance on how to resolve such differences (see especially 15.3). Ultimately the matter may have to be referred to the Court of Protection via the Public Guardian (14.19).

An LPA can be revoked if the donor has capacity to do this (Section 13(2)), even if he may at the time lack capacity to make the decisions the attorney was empowered to make.

Who may be an attorney?

No one can be compelled to act as an attorney under an LPA. The attorney's statement in the LPA confirms that he has read the prescribed information, and understood his duties under the LPA, the Act, and the Code of Practice. In signing he accepts his role. After the LPA has been registered, in order to withdraw from his appointment he must notify the donor, any other attorney and the Office of the Public Guardian, using the prescribed form set out in the Regulations. The Code of Practice gives guidance as to who may be an attorney. An individual has to be named rather than described by reference to a job title. A paid care worker (such as a care home manager) should not agree to act as an attorney, apart from in unusual circumstances (for example, if they are the only close relative of the donor).

The role and duties of an attorney

The duties of an attorney are outlined at 7.58 of the Code of Practice and include a duty of care in decision-making, a duty to act in good faith and not take advantage of his position, and a duty to carry out the donor's instructions and to respect his confidentiality. The section 44 criminal offence of ill-treatment or neglect is specifically applied to attorneys, including those appointed under an EPA. Even where the decision does not fall clearly within his authority under the LPA, an attorney has a right to be consulted when the decision-maker is applying the best interests checklist under s 4.

Advance decisions and Lasting Powers of Attorney

The relationship between advance decisions and Lasting Powers of Attorney covering personal welfare issues might cause some difficulties in practice. If the advance decision was made after the appointment of an attorney then the attorney could not consent to treatment specifically refused by the advance decision. If the LPA had been made later then, as discussed above, the issue would be whether the scope of the attorney's authority included consenting to treatments refused in the advance directive. It may be advisable to destroy any earlier advance decisions in case the doctor was unaware of the appointment of an attorney under an LPA. Even where the statement or expression of the person's wishes fell short of constituting a valid and applicable advance decision the attorney would have to bear those wishes in mind when applying the best interests checklist. Similar principles would apply if the Court of Protection had appointed a deputy with powers to decide personal welfare including healthcare issues.

Does the law limit the powers of an attorney?

There are a number of limitations on the powers of an attorney imposed either by the Act itself or the general law. So in the same way that a donor, when he had capacity, could not directly require a healthcare professional to give specific medical treatment (although he could of course refuse such treatment), he could not in the LPA authorise his attorney to require such treatment. Further the Act does not apply to treatment for mental disorder regulated under Part 4 of the Mental Health Act (see Chapter 15). Therefore an attorney could not consent to or refuse such treatment in respect of a formally detained patient. On the other hand he would have authority in relation to treatments for physical conditions or treatment for mental disorder not regulated under Part 4. Where the donor has been made subject to a Guardianship Order under the Mental Health Act the Attorney will not be able to make decisions which conflict with those of the Guardian. However if authorised under the LPA he will be able to exercise the donor's rights under the Mental Health Act, such as applying to a Mental Health Review Tribunal (MHRT). It may also be appropriate in some circumstances to involve the attorney in section 117 aftercare planning.

The role and powers of the Court of Protection

As already mentioned among other obligations, an attorney must follow the best interests checklist in deciding how to act where the donor is incapable of deciding for himself. The fact that the attorney is effectively the designated decision-maker in areas within the scope of the LPA does not absolve others from challenging his decision if they believe that it is not in the donor's best interests. The Court of Protection, through the Office of the Public Guardian, exercises jurisdiction over attorneys.

The Court's powers are set out in ss 22–23 and include:

- deciding whether the formal requirements for the creation of an LPA have been met;

- deciding whether an LPA has been revoked;

- deciding whether fraud or undue influence has been exerted over the creation or execution of the LPA, and if so whether to revoke it or not to register it;

- deciding the meaning or effect of an LPA;

- giving authority to the attorney to make decisions, including gifts which fall outside the scope of the LPA;

- giving directions such as to produce records, accounts or information; or directions in respect of the remuneration or expenses of the attorney, or even to relieve the attorney from liability arising from a breach of his duties.

The Code of Practice advises (7.70–72) that, where abuse or exploitation of the donor by the attorney is suspected, this should be reported to the Office of the Public Guardian, which may refer the matter to the Court of Protection. In the case of a personal welfare LPA covering consent to or refusal of medical treatment, if healthcare professionals disagree with the attorney's decision and are unable to persuade him to a different view they can apply to the Court of Protection and in the meantime under s 6(7) give life-sustaining treatment or treatment which prevents a deterioration, while the court decides the matter. This almost certainly creates a professional obligation to do so. An attorney will himself be protected from liability where an LPA was not effective because, for example, it had been incorrectly created or had been subsequently revoked without his knowledge (s 14(2)). In such circumstances a transaction between the attorney and a third party could be as valid as if the LPA had been effective.

Transitional arrangements for Enduring Powers of Attorney (EPAs)

It has not been possible to make any new EPAs since 1 October 2007. However existing EPAs will continue until the last donor dies. They will not automatically be extended to include additional areas of decision-making which could have been covered by an LPA. If the donor retains capacity and wishes to cover, for example, personal welfare decisions he will have to make an LPA. Existing EPAs will remain valid and will require to be registered with the Office of the Public Guardian when the donor loses capacity. Schedule 4 to the Act essentially reproduces the provisions of the Enduring Powers of Attorney Act 1985. Schedules 7 and 8 to the Lasting Powers of Attorney, Enduring Powers of Attorney and Public Guardian Regulations specify the Notice of Intention to apply for registration of an EPA and the application to register.

Key points and questions relating to Lasting Powers of Attorney

- What area of decision-making does the person wish to cover?

- Does the LPA cover this area of decision-making?

- Have the formal requirements been met?

- If personal welfare LPA is intended to cover medical treatment decisions, does the donor understand what this includes?

- How old is the donor/attorney? They must both be at least 18.
- The LPA does not bypass best interests checklist and s 1 principles.
- Has the donor of a personal welfare LPA become incapacitated?
- Can the donor make the relevant decision for himself?
- Does the LPA cover the same ground as an advance decision?
- Is the attorney failing to act in the best interests of the donor, or abusing him?

Chapter 9

Deputies and declarations (sections 15–21)

General

The nature, structure and procedural rules of the Court of Protection are dealt with in Chapter 12. The present chapter will cover the powers of the Court of Protection to make declarations, decisions and to appoint deputies. It will also deal with the approach of the court to the use of its powers. One of the main benefits of the Act is to introduce a single court with the power to deal with all issues concerning people who lack or may lack capacity, whether the issue concerns property and affairs or personal welfare and medical decisions. Not only will there no longer be doubt as to which court should be approached, but also issues concerning the limits to the court's powers and to its willingness to become involved should no longer arise. Appeals to the inherent jurisdiction of the court to fill gaps in the law should in future be unnecessary. With the appointment of specialist judges a body of consistent decision-making should emerge in due course. Further, although the introduction of the Court of Protection with its greatly increased powers means that a further possible route to action will become available for health and social care professionals, s 21 provides for the ease of transfer of proceedings between courts where appropriate if the wrong choice is made.

The power to make declarations

As a branch of the High Court of Justice the Court of Protection has power to make declarations and this is confirmed by s 15(1) which provides that it may make declarations as to:

(a) *whether a person has or lacks capacity to make a decision specified in the declaration;*

(b) *whether a person has or lacks capacity to make decisions on such matters as are described in the declaration;*

It would be appropriate to ask the court for a declaration in circumstances where despite following the procedures set out in the Act and the guidance contained in the Code of Practice the decision-maker finds it impossible to reach a conclusion as to whether the person had capacity or not. It would not be appropriate to ask for a declaration simply to provide reassurance to the health or social care professional, but only where there is genuine doubt about a person's capacity. Professionals might disagree about the patient's capacity to consent to a medical procedure, or there might be dispute between family members, or the person concerned might wish to challenge a decision that he lacked capacity (made perhaps by an attorney under an LPA) (see Code of Practice 8.16).

Section 15(1) also provides that the court may make declarations as to:

> (c) *the lawfulness or otherwise of any act done, or to be done, in relation to that person.*

In this context an 'act' would include an omission to act and a course of conduct (s 15(2)). Historically the power of the High Court to make a declaration has been used in relation to controversial areas of medical decision-making. So where there was doubt as to whether a form of treatment should be given or withheld from a person who lacked capacity a declaration would be sought as to whether to proceed in the way desired by the healthcare professionals would be lawful. Section 15 therefore preserves the right of a healthcare professional to apply to the court in such circumstances. The Code of Practice suggests (8.18) that case law in this field arising before the Act will continue to apply. This would mean, for example, that before withdrawing artificial nutrition and hydration from a persistent vegetative state patient an application would need to be made to the court for a declaration that this would be lawful. Other issues which would need to go to court would be the non-therapeutic sterilisation of an adult with learning disabilities, or the issue whether an incapacitated adult could become an organ donor. While this may be so, and declarations may be sought, the power of substituted decision-making by the court introduced by s 16 (see below) may be preferred in future because of the greater degree of certainty conveyed.

The power to make decisions

While the distinction between the court making a declaration as to the lawfulness of an act in relation to a person lacking capacity on the one hand and making the decision on behalf of that person on the other would appear to be somewhat technical, the reality is that it goes to the heart of one of the more controversial elements of the Act, namely the introduction of substituted decision-making. In the past while the court might make a declaration that were a doctor to perform a particular procedure in relation to an incapacitated patient that would be lawful, it would not be *consenting* to the procedure on behalf of the patient. Under a personal welfare LPA a person can appoint an attorney to make medical decisions for him. Under s 16 the Court of Protection can similarly make a medical decision for an incapacitated person as opposed to simply declaring that a particular procedure would be lawful.

If a person lacks capacity in relation either to a personal welfare or property and affairs matter s 16 (2) provides that the court may:

> (a) *by making an order, make the decision or decisions on the person's behalf in relation to the matter or matters, or*

> (b) *appoint a person (a 'deputy') to make decisions on the person's behalf in relation to the matter or matters.*

Examples of decisions that the court might make are given in the Code of Practice: terminating a tenancy agreement, making a will, deciding on the validity of an advance decision, deciding upon a medical procedure, or preventing an individual from contacting a person who lacks capacity. As seen in Chapter 8 the Court of Protection has specific powers to determine the validity and operation of LPAs. From these examples alone it can be seen that there is a fine line between applying for a declaration under s 15 and asking the court to make a decision under s 16.

The approach of the court

In making decisions under s 16, subs 3 provides that the powers of the court are subject to the provisions of the Act and in particular to s 1 (the principles) and s 4 (best interests). So for example the court will start from the presumption that the person has capacity to make the decision for himself and in reaching its conclusion will apply both the definition of incapacity and the test for incapacity under ss 2 and 3. If it reaches the conclusion that the person lacks capacity in relation to the decision in question and that there are no practical steps which might be taken to allow the person to achieve capacity to make the decision for himself, it will go through the requirements of the best interests checklist under s 4, consulting where appropriate, seeking to establish what is known of the person's own wishes, and applying the principle of equal consideration.

We have already seen that under s 16 the court may make a decision itself or appoint a deputy (see later) to make the decision or decisions. The default position however is that the court should make the decision, requiring the applicant to return to the court should another decision be needed in the future. Section 16(4) provides that a decision by the court is to be preferred to the appointment of a deputy and that where a deputy *is* appointed the powers conferred on him should be as limited in scope and duration as is reasonably practicable in the circumstances. This is in keeping with the section 1(6) principle that regard must be had to whether the necessary purpose can be as effectively achieved in a way that is less restrictive of the person's rights and freedom of action. In other words the court will intervene to the least extent necessary rather than the most that it can.

Personal welfare decisions

The powers of the court to make personal welfare decisions are not exhaustively set out, but s 17 gives examples as follows:

- deciding where the person is to live;

- deciding what contact, if any, the person is to have with any specified persons;

- making an order prohibiting a named person from having contact with the person;

- giving or refusing consent to the carrying out or continuation of a treatment by a person providing health care for the person;

- giving a direction that a person responsible for the person's health care allow a different person to take over that responsibility.

These are wide powers which would include providing authority for a person to deprive an incapacitated person of liberty within the meaning of Article 5 of the European Convention on Human Rights, where this cannot be authorised as a section 5 act because of the limitations imposed by s 6 (see Chapter 7). This is also spelled out in the amendments to the Act made by the Mental Health Act 2007 (new S4A(3),(4)); but the court's powers will be limited in that it will not be able to make an order depriving a person lacking capacity of liberty where he is ineligible under the *Bournewood* safeguards (see Chapter 16)

Property and affairs decisions

There is similarly no exhaustive list of the section 16 powers of the court in relation to an incapacitated person's property and affairs. However s 18 provides examples closely modelled on the Mental Health Act s 96 powers of the existing Court of Protection, i.e.:

- the control and management of the person's property;

- the sale, exchange, charging, gift or other disposition of the person's property;

- the acquisition of property in the person's name or on the person's behalf;

- the carrying on, on a person's behalf, of any profession, trade or business;

- the taking of a decision which will have the effect of dissolving a partnership of which the person is a member;

- the carrying out of any contract entered into by the person;

- the discharge of the person's debts and of any of the person's obligations, whether legally enforceable or not;

- the settlement of any of the person's property, whether for the person's benefit or for the benefit of others;

- the execution for the person of a will;

- the exercise of any power (including a power to consent) vested in the person whether beneficially or as trustee or otherwise;

- the conduct of legal proceedings in the person's name or on a person's behalf.

The court's powers extend to those under the age of 16 if the court considers it likely that the person will still lack capacity to make such decisions when he reaches his age of 18. This is an exception to the general rule that the Act applies only to those aged 16 and above.

The power to appoint a deputy

We have already seen that the court has power under s 16 to appoint a deputy to make decisions on behalf of a person who lacks capacity, but that the starting point for the court will be that it should make the decision for itself and that where it does appoint a deputy it will limit the scope and duration of the appointment. Section 16(8) provides that:

The court may, in particular, revoke the appointment of a deputy or vary the powers conferred on him if it is satisfied that the deputy –

(a) *has behaved, or is behaving, in a way that contravenes the authority conferred on him by the court or is not in the person's best interests, or*

(b) *proposes to behave in a way that would contravene that authority or would not be in the person's best interests.*

The old Court of Protection frequently appointed receivers to manage the property and affairs of a person who lacked capacity. What is new in the Act is that a deputy may be appointed both in respect of property and affairs issues and/or personal welfare issues. The deputy must be over 18 or in the case of property and affairs issues could also be a trust corporation such as a bank or other financial institution. A deputy would naturally have to consent to his appointment. Two or more deputies may be appointed to act jointly or jointly and severally. They can even be appointed to act jointly in respect of some matters and jointly and severally in respect of others. When appointing a deputy the court may at the same time appoint a successor to a take over in specified circumstances, for example where the deputy appointed dies or himself becomes incapable of acting. Deputies can claim reasonable expenses from the estate of the person lacking capacity and may be given power by the court to deal with the control and management of property, including the power to invest. He may be required to give security for his conduct and to submit reports to the Public Guardian.

The Code of Practice gives guidance at 8.32–33 as to the kind of person who might be appointed a deputy. Clearly the court will have in mind the nature of the decisions the deputy is empowered to make, whether concerning property and affairs or personal welfare. While a family member may be appropriate in relation to personal welfare issues, the court could appoint a professional deputy in relation to complex financial issues.

When might a deputy be appointed?

For issues concerning property and affairs a deputy is likely to be appointed in similar circumstances to the current appointment of receivers. So this will be largely unnecessary where the person has no property or assets, but merely social security benefits. It is more difficult to decide when it would be appropriate to apply for a deputy to be appointed in respect of the new area of personal welfare decisions. A deputy would not be needed to make ordinary care and treatment decisions because those would be covered as section 5 acts, needing no specific additional authority. However it may be appropriate:

● if that person had complex medical needs which would be likely to require repeated difficult treatment decisions to be made over a period of time;

● where family members were repeatedly unable to agree among themselves over what was in that person's best interests;

● where there were regular irreconcilable differences between the health and social care professionals and the family or friends of the person concerned.

What restrictions affect a deputy's powers?

The overriding restriction on a deputy is that at all times he must act in accordance with the powers specifically given to him by the court and cannot exceed those powers without first going back to the court for extended authority. Section 20 sets out specific limitations on a deputy's powers:

- a deputy cannot act in relation to a matter if he knows or has reasonable grounds for believing that a person has capacity in relation to that matter. The fact that a deputy has been appointed does not mean that he is free to make decisions even in relation to areas given to him by the court if the person has capacity to make the decision himself. His authority is to be exercised in keeping with the provisions of the Act and in particular the section 1 principles and section 4 best interests checklist. So the deputy would, amongst other things, have to apply the functional test, (i.e., has *this* person capacity to make *this* decision *now*), consider what practical steps could be taken to assist the person making the decision for himself, and consider whether the decision could safely be put back until a time when the person could make it himself. If the person lacked capacity the deputy, in following the best interests checklist, would have to consult as required and apply the principle of equal consideration.

- The court cannot give a deputy power to prohibit a named person from having contact with the person, nor to require a person responsible for his health care to allow a different person to take over that responsibility. The court has such powers but they cannot be granted to a deputy.

- In the area of property and affairs a deputy may not be given power to settle any of the person's property, nor to execute a will on his behalf nor exercise any power vested in him.

- A deputy may not be given power which conflicts with a decision made within the scope of his authority by an attorney or attorneys under an LPA.

- A deputy may not be given power to refuse consent to the carrying out of or continuation of life-sustaining treatment in relation to the person.

- A deputy is subject to the limitations on the use of restraint, and the prohibition against deprivation of liberty set out in s 6 (see Chapter 7). In addition any use of restraint must fall within the scope of the authority conferred on him by the court. On the other hand where a deputy meets these conditions and is authorised to act in relation to the matter by the court this would prevent anyone else relying on s 5 to make the decision.

- Although a deputy, if given the power by the court, may exercise some of a detained patient's rights under the Mental Health Act on his behalf such as the right to apply to a Mental Health Review Tribunal, he could not consent or refuse treatment for mental disorder regulated under Part 4 of the Mental Health Act, nor make decisions (for example about where the person should live) which conflict with a Guardianship order (see Chapter 15).

The responsibilities and duties of a deputy

In addition to acting in accordance with the s 1 principles and s 4 best interests checklist dealt with above, a deputy is specifically required to have regard to the guidance contained in the Code of Practice by s 42(4). He must also always act within the limits of the authority conferred on him by the court. The Code of Practice at 8.56 summarises the duties of a deputy, in keeping with the law of agency which by s 19(6) is specifically applied to deputies, as follows, to:

- *act with due care and skill (duty of care)*
- *not take advantage of their situation (fiduciary duty)*
- *indemnify the person against liability to third parties caused by the deputy's negligence*
- *not delegate their duties unless authorised to do so*
- *act in good faith*
- *respect the person's confidentiality, and*
- *comply with the directions of the Court of Protection*

In relation to property and affairs, they also have a duty to keep accounts and keep the person's money and property separate from their own finances.

The Court of Protection, through the Office of the Public Guardian, exercises control over deputies. Anyone who has concern about the manner in which a deputy is exercising his powers should report the matter to the Public Guardian. The Court of Protection can revoke the appointment or amend the powers given to the deputy. The offence under s 44 of ill-treatment or neglect of a person who lacks capacity is specifically applied to court-appointed deputies.

Key points and questions relating to the Court of Protection and deputies

- The Court of Protection deals with all issues concerning an incapacitated person.
- The court can make *declarations* as to incapacity or the lawfulness of actions.
- The court can make *decisions* on behalf of an incapacitated person.
- The court is governed by the best interests checklist and s 1 principles.
- The court will prefer to make the decision itself rather than appoint a deputy.
- The court controls the appointment, actions and powers of a deputy.
- Deputies cannot make decisions where the person retains capacity.
- Deputies must have regard to the Code of Practice and follow the best interests checklist and s 1 principles.

Chapter 10
Advance decisions to refuse treatment (sections 24–26)

General

It is a curious feature of much of the media reporting of the Mental Capacity Act that it has focused on one part which in fact introduces very little change to the existing law but which is presented as being one of its more controversial innovations. Advance decisions to refuse treatment, 'living wills', or advance refusals represent a long-established feature of the common law. An adult of sound mind is entitled to refuse medical treatment, whether face to face with the healthcare professional or in advance, anticipating a time when the person may lack capacity to refuse the treatment in question. This is a right protected by Article 8 of the European Convention on Human Rights. The provisions relating to advance decisions to refuse treatment in the Mental Capacity Act are largely a replication and codification of the common law, which is why their description as introducing the concept of preventing a doctor from giving certain treatments, including end-of-life treatments, is unfortunate.

The statutory provisions

The provisions are contained within ss 24–26 of the Mental Capacity Act.

Section 24 defines an advance decision (the somewhat misleading shorthand term used in the Act itself) as follows:

(1) *'Advance decision' means a decision made by a person ('P'), after he has reached 18 and when he has capacity to do so, that if –*

    (a) *at a later time and in such circumstances as he may specify, specified treatment is proposed to be carried out or continued by a person providing health care for him, and*

    (b) *at that time he lacks capacity to consent to the carrying out or continuation of the treatment,*

the specified treatment is not to be carried out or continued.

Note that the provision relates only to the *refusal* of treatment. An advance decision cannot bind a healthcare professional to *give* specified treatment any more than a competent patient can require such treatment face to face. Note also that an advance decision is limited to a refusal of a specified *treatment given by a person providing health care*. It does not cover refusals of other acts. So a person could not therefore make a binding advance decision to refuse to be admitted, for example, to a particular care home. A person's wishes in relation to issues outside the field of health care could of course be incorporated in a written statement, which the decision-maker would have to bear in mind (but would not be bound by) when deciding best interests under s 4. Even within the field of health care it is not possible by an advance decision to refuse consent to the provision of basic care, including nursing care, which may therefore always lawfully be given.

Section 24 further provides that layman's terms may be used, and that if the person retains capacity he may withdraw or alter (not necessarily in writing) the advance decision. The Code of Practice (9.21; 9.23; 9.31) emphasises that, particularly where an advance decision or its withdrawal is verbal, this should be documented by the healthcare professional.

An advance decision must be valid

To be effective an advance decision must be *valid* and *applicable*. This is explained in s 25. An advance decision will not be *valid*

- if the person has withdrawn it, although he must of course have capacity to do so at the time.

- if the person has subsequently made a Lasting Power of Attorney in which the attorney is authorised to give or refuse consent to the treatment covered by the advance decision. It may not be a straightforward matter to decide whether the attorney's authority does indeed relate to the treatment in question as there may be two documents couched in very different language; in fact the advance decision may not be in writing at all.

- if the person has subsequently acted inconsistently. So for example a person may have made an advance decision to refuse blood products. If six months later, while still retaining capacity, he accepts blood products, that would be 'clearly inconsistent with the advance decision remaining his fixed decision' (s 25(2)(c)).

An advance decision must be applicable

An advance decision will not be *applicable*

- if the treatment is not the treatment specified. This sounds obvious but could give rise to difficulties in practice. A judge would be reluctant to extend the scope of an advance decision on the basis that 'I am sure he meant to include that treatment as well'.

- if the person has capacity at the time to give or refuse consent; if that is the case it is the patient whom the healthcare professional consults and not his written advance decision!

- if any specified circumstances are absent or if there are reasonable grounds for believing that circumstances exist which the person did not anticipate at the time and which would have affected his decision. This would cover a situation where consent to specific treatment had been refused in an advance decision based on then current medical knowledge and practice, which significantly changed after he lost capacity. Keyhole surgery might have become possible, or new drug therapies available without the side effects the person particularly wished to avoid.

What are the formal requirements?

In most circumstances no particular formality is required for an advance decision. It may be in writing, verbal, signed, unsigned, dated, undated, witnessed, not witnessed. If it is in writing the Code of Practice (9.19) suggests that it should contain:

- full details of the person making the advance decision, including date of birth, home address and any distinguishing features (in case healthcare professionals need to identify an unconscious person, for example);

- the name and address of the person's GP and whether they have a copy of the document;

- a statement that the document should be used if the person ever lacks capacity to make treatment decisions;

- a clear statement of the decision, the treatment to be refused and the circumstances in which the decision will apply;

- the date the document was written (or reviewed);

- the person's signature (or the signature of someone the person has asked to sign on their behalf and in their presence);

- the signature of the person witnessing the signature, if there is one (or a statement directing somebody to sign on the person's behalf).

Contrast this advice with the complex and very specific formal *requirements* for a Lasting Power of Attorney.

There is one significant change introduced by the Mental Capacity Act where the advance decision is to apply to life-sustaining treatment. In these circumstances it must be verified by a statement by the person that it is to apply to that treatment even if his life is at risk. It must also be in writing, signed by the person or by another person in his presence and at his direction, and the signature made or acknowledged by the person in the presence of a witness who himself signs it or acknowledges his signature in the person's presence (s 25(5)(6)). This is an important change in the law because many advance decisions do relate to life-sustaining treatment. Life-sustaining treatment is rather unhelpfully defined in s 4(10) as 'treatment which in the view of a person providing health care for the person concerned is necessary to sustain life'. It could include resuscitation, artificial nutrition and hydration, or even antibiotics.

There are transitional arrangements where an advance decision covering life-sustaining treatment has been made before 1 October 2007 but does not meet these formal requirements. These arrangements are introduced by article 5 of the Mental Capacity Act 2005 (Transitional and Consequential Provisions) Order 2007 (SI 2007 No. 1898) and provide that if such an advance decision has been made and the person lacks capacity since 1 October 2007 to comply with the new requirements then so long as it is in writing and is otherwise valid and applicable it does not need to satisfy the requirements of verification, nor of being signed and witnessed.

The effect of a valid and applicable advance decision

Where an advance decision is both valid and applicable its effect is as if a capacitated adult had decided against a form of treatment in person and at the relevant time. It could not be overturned, even by the Court of Protection. Furthermore the s 1 principle of assumption of capacity will apply, so that it will be for the person seeking to displace an advance decision to prove that it is either not valid or not applicable.

If it is valid and applicable this will be conclusive as to the best interests of an incapacitated person. This needs to be borne in mind when the decision-maker is considering the best interests checklist under s 4. Further, treatment could not legitimately be given with the protection of a s 5 defence in the face of a valid and applicable advance decision to the contrary.

Protection for healthcare professionals (see also Chapter 7)

In keeping with similar provisions elsewhere in the Act there is protection given depending upon whether a person believes that an advance decision either does or does not exist in relation to the proposed treatment. So a person does not incur liability for treating a patient unless he is satisfied that there is a valid and applicable advance decision in existence, which relates to that treatment and nevertheless proceeds to give it. On the other hand a person does not incur liability if he withholds or withdraws treatment from a patient where he reasonably believes that a valid and applicable advance decision covering the treatment exists. If the decision-maker suspects that an advance decision exists he must make reasonable efforts, time permitting, to find out what it says. The Code of Practice (9.49) suggests this might include discussions with relatives, looking in the clinical records or contacting the person's GP. An emergency might rule out or strictly limit such 'reasonable efforts'.

Problems in practice

Although the law relating to advance decisions is relatively simple a number of problems can present in practice. There may be a question as to whether the person had capacity at the time of making or withdrawing it; there may be conflicting evidence as to whether the person subsequently changed his mind or whether medical developments would have affected his decision. Relatives consulted may have differing perceptions of what the person intended. It may be difficult to establish whether the wording used by the person covers the scenario in question; would an advance decision made by a woman continue to apply were she to become pregnant? There may be suspicions that undue influence might have been exerted on the person. The case of *Re T* (Adult: Refusal of Medical Treatment) [1992] 4 All ER 649, rehearses a large number of such issues and was decided on a different basis respectively by the High Court and by the Court of Appeal. The judgment repays careful reading in relation to what might vitiate an apparently effective advance decision. An advance decision may not be what it at first sight appears.

The question will always arise as to how far the decision-maker has to go to establish the existence, validity and applicability of an advance decision. There is no requirement to assume the existence of an advance decision and obsessive efforts to trace an advance decision in circumstances where, even if time permits, there is no suggestion that the patient made one, are not required. However, where the decision-maker suspects that an advance decision exists, then, time permitting, he will be obliged to establish the true position. It is part of the best interests checklist that the decision-maker must consider 'so far as is reasonably ascertainable' the person's past and present wishes and feelings (and in particular, any relevant written statement made by him when he had capacity) (s 4(6)). If, however, there is a valid and applicable advance decision, that will displace consideration of the best interests checklist and will be regarded as conclusive evidence of the person's binding decision.

Even with reasonable efforts there may be circumstances in which it is far from clear whether an advance decision is valid or applicable or indeed exists at all. Section 26 provides that a declaration may be sought from the Court of Protection on such an issue and that while the court's decision is being sought, life-sustaining treatment or actions reasonably believed to be necessary to prevent a serious deterioration in the patient's condition may be performed without incurring liability.

Advance decisions refusing treatment for mental disorder

What is the situation in respect of a person who makes an advance decision to refuse treatment for mental disorder? There is no reason why under the Mental Capacity Act such an advance decision should not be both valid and applicable. So a patient having made an advance decision to refuse ECT could not, if subsequently admitted to hospital informally and at a time when he had lost capacity, have ECT imposed upon him. However, s 28 provides that the Act does not apply to people detained under the Mental Health Act whose treatment is being regulated under Part 4 and therefore any advance decision by such a person to refuse such treatment will not be applicable. This is logical because a person detained under the formal provisions of the Mental Health Act who retains capacity can have treatment regulated by Part 4 imposed on him under ss 58 and 63 despite his competent refusal, provided of course that the necessary formal requirements are met. It would be strange if such treatment could be refused in advance but not at the time. However, such an advance decision would have to be considered as a statement of the person's wishes when decisions as to treatment in that person's best interests were being made, even though it would not be binding.

The Mental Capacity Act applies to a patient formally detained under the Mental Health Act other than in respect of Part 4 treatment so that, for example, treatments proposed for physical conditions would be governed by Mental Capacity Act principles and a relevant advance decision would be applicable; likewise treatments even for mental disorder where a patient is held under a short-term provision of the Mental Health Act such as s 5 or s 4.

Advance decisions and Lasting Powers of Attorney

The relationship between advance decisions and Lasting Powers of Attorney covering personal welfare issues may cause some difficulties in practice. If the advance decision was made after the appointment of an attorney then the attorney could not consent to treatment specifically refused by the advance decision. If the LPA had been made later then, as discussed above, the issue would be whether the scope of the attorney's authority included consenting to treatments refused in the advance decision. Even where the statement or expression of the person's wishes fell short of constituting a valid and applicable advance decision the attorney would have to bear those wishes in mind when applying the best interests checklist. Similar principles would apply if the Court of Protection had appointed a deputy with powers to decide personal welfare including healthcare issues.

Conscientious objections by healthcare professionals

Section 62 confirms for the avoidance of doubt that nothing in the Mental Capacity Act is to be taken to affect the law relating to murder, manslaughter or assisted suicide. An advance decision, which by definition covers only *refusals* of treatment, would be unlikely to raise such issues. But what if the healthcare professional cannot for reasons of conscience comply with an advance decision to refuse life-sustaining treatment? His rights in this respect are protected by Article 9 of the European Convention on Human Rights which covers freedom of thought, conscience and religion. In such circumstances the patient cannot simply be abandoned, nor can the healthcare professional be required to act against his or her conscience. Attempts must be made to transfer the care of the patient to another healthcare professional and in case of difficulty application can be made to the Court of Protection, which has specific power under s 17(1)(e) to direct someone else to take over responsibility for the patient's care.

Key points and questions relating to advance decisions

- If the advance decision is to refuse life-sustaining treatment, does it meet the formal requirements?

- Did the person have capacity when making the advance decision?

- Is there any evidence of a change of mind or of withdrawal?

- Is there any significant change of circumstances which may have affected the person's decision?

- Does the advance decision clearly cover the treatment in question?

- Did the person mean the advance decision to apply in these circumstances?

- Even if it does not meet the requirements for an advance decision it may still be a statement of wishes to be considered under s 4.

- An advance decision trumps the best interests checklist.

- An advance decision does not cover treatment regulated by Part 4 of the Mental Health Act 1983.

- Is there an LPA covering the same circumstances?

Chapter 11

Independent Mental Capacity Advocates (IMCAs) (sections 35–41)

Introduction

The Independent Mental Capacity Advocacy Service was a late addition to the Act. The Joint Parliamentary Committee received considerable volumes of evidence that there was a need for independent advocacy to be available to assist people with capacity problems to make and communicate decisions. The Government accepted the Committee's recommendation and so advocacy is included in the Act. The IMCA service has been available since April 2007 in England and since October 2007 in Wales. Practitioners should already be aware of how to contact the service. It should be noted that the service is limited to specific situations and that the amount of time allocated for an IMCA to make a particular decision is also limited.

Most people who lack capacity to make an important decision (for example, about treatment or where to live) will have family or friends who will be consulted by any decision-maker because of the requirements of the Mental Capacity Act. The IMCA service is for people who lack such people to help represent them.

Purpose of the service

Section 35 of the Act sets out the principle and purpose of the IMCA:

(1) The appropriate authority must make such arrangements as it considers reasonable to enable persons ('independent mental capacity advocates') to be available to represent and support persons to whom acts or decisions proposed under ss 37, 38 and 39 relate.

(4) In making arrangements under subsection (1), the appropriate authority must have regard to the principle that a person to whom a proposed act or decision relates should, so far as practicable, be represented and supported by a person who is independent of any person who will be responsible for the act or decision.

Money has been allocated to local authorities (in England) or health boards (in Wales) to allow them to commission advocacy services. These have mostly been provided by existing advocacy services who have then organised themselves to be able to take on this function. They have been required to appoint only people who have been trained to provide what is, in effect, non-instructional or 'best interests' advocacy. This is where an advocate represents what he or she considers a person's wishes would be, if they were able to express them. This is a specialist area, as most advocates are used to working with people who can clearly express what they want.

The main circumstances where an IMCA should be appointed have been set out below. The role of the IMCA is to support and represent the person concerned, to ascertain their wishes and feelings and to check that the Act's principles and best interests checklist are followed. The IMCA cannot veto certain decisions but the relevant authority must take into account any information or submissions provided by the IMCA. If they are very concerned that the person's best interests were not being followed the IMCA could challenge a decision by going to the Court of Protection.

The role of the IMCA is summarised by the Code of Practice at Chapter 10 as:

> *to help particularly vulnerable people who lack the capacity to make important decisions about serious medical treatment and changes of accommodation, and who have no family or friends that it would be appropriate to consult about those decisions. IMCAs will work with and support people who lack capacity, and represent their views to those who are working out their best interests.*

Powers of the advocate

The Act confers certain powers on the IMCA to enable them to carry out their role effectively. Section 35 states that:

> (6) *For the purpose of enabling him to carry out his functions, an independent mental capacity advocate –*
>
> > (a) *may interview in private the person whom he has been instructed to represent, and*
> >
> > (b) *may, at all reasonable times, examine and take copies of –*
> >
> > > (i) *any health record,*
> > >
> > > (ii) *any record of, or held by, a local authority and compiled in connection with a social services function, and*
> > >
> > > (iii) *any record held by a person registered under Part 2 of the Care Standards Act 2000 (c. 14),*
> >
> > *which the person holding the record considers may be relevant to the independent mental capacity advocate's investigation.*

This statutory right of access to records is very significant in strengthening the position of the IMCA. Section 36 states that the accompanying Regulations should identify how the IMCA should carry out their primary functions of:

(2)(a) *providing support to the person whom he has been instructed to represent ('P') so that P may participate as fully as possible in any relevant decision;*

(b) *obtaining and evaluating relevant information;*

(c) *ascertaining what P's wishes and feelings would be likely to be, and the beliefs and values that would be likely to influence P, if he had capacity;*

(d) *ascertaining what alternative courses of action are available in relation to P;*

(e) *obtaining a further medical opinion where treatment is proposed and the advocate thinks that one should be obtained.*

The Regulations also make provision as to circumstances in which the advocate may challenge, or provide assistance for the purpose of challenging, any relevant decision.

England's Regulations are available at:

www.opsi.gov.uk/si/si2006/20061832.htm

The Regulations for Wales are available at:

www.opsi.gov.uk/legislation/wales/wsi2007/20070852e.htm

(Note that these addresses are at slight variance with those given in the Code of Practice as they were giving more direct access as this book went to print. In case of difficulty enter 'mental capacity act regulations' in your search engine.)

The need for an IMCA

1. Provision of serious medical treatment by an NHS body

Section 37 requires an NHS body to instruct an IMCA to represent a person if:

(i) it is proposing to provide serious medical treatment for that person;

(ii) the person lacks capacity to consent to the treatment, and

(iii) it is satisfied that there is no-one, other than one engaged in providing care or treatment for them in a professional capacity or for remuneration, whom it would be appropriate to consult in determining what would be in the person's best interests.

This would apply to someone who had no suitable family or friends to consult (plus no-one granted LPA, etc., see list of exceptions below).

This section does not apply if the person's treatment is regulated by Part 4 of the Mental Health Act. This has its own set of rules and requirements for consultation.

If the treatment needs to be provided as a matter of urgency, it may be provided even though the NHS body has not been able to instruct an IMCA.

The IMCA cannot block the provision of treatment but the NHS body must take into account any information given, or submissions made, by them.

'Serious medical treatment' means treatment which involves providing, withholding or withdrawing treatment of a kind prescribed by regulations made by the appropriate authority.

The Mental Capacity Act 2005 (Independent Mental Capacity Advocates) (General) Regulations (2006, No. 1832) at 4(2) describes serious medical treatment as:

> *treatment which involves providing, withdrawing or withholding treatment in circumstances where –*
>
> *(a) in a case where a single treatment is being proposed, there is a fine balance between its benefits to the patient and the burdens and risks it is likely to entail for him,*
>
> *(b) in a case where there is a choice of treatments, a decision as to which one to use is finely balanced, or*
>
> *(c) what is proposed would be likely to involve serious consequences for the patient.*

Point (b) is somewhat surprising and may lead to some debate concerning what are relatively minor procedures but where there is a choice of treatments and where the decision is finely balanced.

Otherwise the decision-maker will find some general guidance in the Code which gives some examples of treatments (para 10.45) that may be considered serious, including:

- *chemotherapy and surgery for cancer;*
- *electro-convulsive therapy;*
- *therapeutic sterilisation;*
- *major surgery (such as open-heart surgery or brain/neuro-surgery);*
- *major amputations (for example, loss of an arm or leg);*
- *treatments which will result in permanent loss of hearing or sight;*
- *withholding or stopping artificial nutrition and hydration; and*
- *termination of pregnancy.*

The Code goes on to state:

> *These are illustrative examples only, and whether these or other procedures are considered serious medical treatment in any given case, will depend on the circumstances and the consequences for the patient. There are also many more treatments which will be defined as serious medical treatments under the Act's Regulations. Decision-makers who are not sure whether they need to instruct an IMCA should consult their colleagues.*

2. Provision of accommodation by an NHS body

Section 38 requires an NHS body to instruct an IMCA to represent a person, if the NHS body proposes to make arrangements:

(i) for the provision of accommodation in a hospital or care home for a person who lacks capacity to agree to the arrangements; or

(ii) for a change in their accommodation to another hospital or care home; and

(iii) it is satisfied that there is no person, other than one engaged in providing care or treatment for them in a professional capacity or for remuneration, whom it would be appropriate for it to consult in determining what would be in the person's best interests.

As with the provision of serious medical treatment, this excludes anyone dealt with compulsorily under the Mental Health Act. An obligation to reside somewhere may be a condition of s 17 leave, guardianship or supervised aftercare (or a Community Treatment Order when this replaces supervised aftercare).

This applies to any accommodation which is likely to last for more than 28 days in a hospital or eight weeks in a care home, but arrangements can be made in an emergency. As noted above, the IMCA should support and represent the person concerned and the authority must take into account any views expressed by them.

3. Provision of accommodation by a local authority

Section 39 requires a local authority to instruct an IMCA to represent a person if the local authority proposes to make arrangements:

(i) for the provision of residential accommodation for a person who lacks capacity to agree to the arrangements; or

(ii) for a change in the person's residential accommodation; and

(iii) it is satisfied that there is no person, other than one engaged in providing care or treatment for them in a professional capacity or for remuneration, whom it would be appropriate for it to consult in determining what would be in the person's best interests.

Again, this excludes anyone dealt with compulsorily under the Mental Health Act. An obligation to reside somewhere may be a condition of s 17 leave, guardianship or supervised aftercare (or a Community Treatment Order when this replaces supervised aftercare).

This applies to any accommodation which is likely to last for more than eight weeks, but arrangements can be made in an emergency.

The section only applies if the accommodation is to be provided in accordance with s 21 or 29 of the National Assistance Act 1948, or s 117 of the Mental Health Act, as the result of a decision taken by the local authority under s 47 of the National Health Service and Community Care Act 1990.

Exceptions: when an IMCA will not be needed

Section 40 means that if someone has been nominated by the person to be consulted in matters affecting his interests, there will be no requirement to instruct an IMCA. This will also be the case if there is:

(i)   a donee of a lasting power of attorney created by P,

(ii) a deputy appointed by the court for P, or

(iii) a donee of an enduring power of attorney (within the meaning of Schedule 4) created by P.

Other circumstances when an IMCA could be involved

Section 41 allowed for the expansion of the IMCA role and this has already happened as a result of revised regulations (SI No. 2883).

There is discretion to appoint an IMCA for care reviews and for adult protection procedures (even if family members are involved). The relevant authority must consider in each individual case whether to appoint an IMCA. There needs to be some benefit from having an IMCA for one to be appointed in these circumstances. The Code of Practice (10.61) suggests that there should be a local policy to cover this area and guidance has been issued. This is available on the Department of Health's website at gateway 7557 and is entitled 'Adult protection, care reviews and Independent Mental Capacity Advocates (IMCA): Guidance on interpreting the regulations extending the IMCA role'.

The role of the IMCA

The Code of Practice (10.20) provides a helpful summary of the IMCA's role. It states that the IMCA should decide how best to represent and support the person who lacks capacity and that they:

- *must confirm that the person instructing them has the authority to do so*
- *should interview or meet in private the person who lacks capacity, if possible*
- *must act in accordance with the principles of the Act (as set out in s 1 of the Act and chapter 2 of the Code) and take account of relevant guidance in the Code*
- *may examine any relevant records that s 35(6) of the Act gives them access to*
- *should get the views of professionals and paid workers providing care or treatment for the person who lacks capacity*
- *should get the views of anybody else who can give information about the wishes and feelings, beliefs or values of the person who lacks capacity*
- *should get hold of any other information they think will be necessary*
- *must find out what support a person who lacks capacity has had to help them make the specific decision*
- *must try to find out what the person's wishes and feelings, beliefs and values would be likely to be if the person had capacity*

- *should find out what alternative options there are*

- *should consider whether getting another medical opinion would help the person who lacks capacity, and*

- *must write a report on their findings for the local authority or NHS body.*

Training and procedures for staff on the role of the IMCA

Health and social services authorities should have procedures, training and awareness programmes to ensure that:

- *all relevant staff know when they need to instruct an IMCA and are able to do so promptly*

- *all relevant staff know how to get in touch with the IMCA service and know the procedure for instructing an IMCA*

- *they record an IMCA's involvement in a case and any information the IMCA provides to help decision-making*

- *they also record how a decision-maker has taken into account the IMCA's report and information as part of the process of working out the person's best interests (this should include reasons for disagreeing with that advice, if relevant)*

- *they give access to relevant records when requested by an IMCA under section 35(6)(b) of the Act*

- *the IMCA gets information about changes that may affect the support and representation the IMCA provides*

- *decision-makers let all relevant people know when an IMCA is working on a person's case, and*

- *decision-makers inform the IMCA of the final decision taken and the reason for it.*

(Code of Practice 10.14)

ACTIVITY **11.1**

Multiple choice questions

Read each question carefully and tick the appropriate box(es). Where a statement is correct, tick the box next to it; if it is incorrect, leave it blank. You may need to tick more than one box per question.

Appendix 5 (pages 145–9) gives the answers.

11.1 The IMCA service:

    (a) is based on a statutory requirement

    (b) uses only qualified solicitors

    (c) aims to represent and support people for particular acts

    (d) provides substituted decision-making in relation to healthcare matters

    (e) may be involved in vulnerable adult procedures

    (f) has the right to interview certain people in private

11.2 IMCAs provide a form of non-instructional advocacy:

    (a) True

    (b) False

11.3 An IMCA has the power to veto any decision made by a local authority or NHS Trust:

    (a) True

    (b) False

Chapter 12

The Court of Protection and the Public Guardian (sections 45–61)

General

Section 45(6) of the Act abolished the previous Court of Protection. Section 45(1) establishes a new court bearing the same name. This is unfortunate because the new court is altogether more powerful and wide-ranging in its powers and scope than the existing court and is not to be confused with it. It has a Central Office, and specialist judges. It will have a regional presence, as the court may sit anywhere in England and Wales on any day at any time (s 45(3)). Any District Registry of the High Court or County Court Office may be designated an additional Registry of the Court of Protection by the Lord Chancellor (s 45(5)).

The Court of Protection deals with all issues concerning people who lack capacity, not merely making orders in respect of their property and affairs but in addition covering issues of personal welfare including the making of medical decisions: from ethical dilemmas posed by novel medical treatments to the investment of assets; from applications to challenge powers being exercised under LPAs to authorising deprivation of liberty; from determining where a person lacking capacity should live and who should have contact with him to appointing someone to consent to or refuse medical treatment on behalf of the incapacitated person. Over time it is to be hoped that the court will develop expertise and a body of precedent, which will inform decision-making respect of people who lack capacity. No longer is it necessary to invoke the inherent jurisdiction of the High Court on welfare issues, relying on it to fill gaps elsewhere in the law relating to decisions that can be made in respect of people who lack capacity. The High Court did not always feel disposed to intervene in these situations.

The powers of the Court of Protection, and the principles which guide the use of those powers (such as the requirement to follow the best interests checklist of s 4) are set out in ss 15–23 (see Chapters 8 and 9). This chapter deals with the court process and functions, together with the role of the Public Guardian, who is in many ways its gatekeeper, executive arm and public face.

The court structure

The judges of the Court of Protection will be nominated by the Lord Chancellor and must be either the President of the Family Division, the Vice-Chancellor, a High Court, Circuit or

District Judge. One of the senior nominated judges will be designated President and another Vice-President of the Court of Protection. Section 47 provides that the court has the same powers, rights, privileges and authority as the High Court. These include High Court powers in relation to witnesses, contempt of court, and enforcement of its orders. Section 48 provides that the court will have power to make interim orders or directions if there is reason to believe that the person lacks capacity in relation to the matter in question, that the matter is one to which the court powers under this Act extend, and that it is in the person's best interests to make the order or give the directions without delay. In order to discharge its functions the court can call for reports covering whatever it directs, from the Public Guardian or from Court of Protection Visitors, or if necessary requiring a local authority or NHS body to arrange for such reports to be made. The report may be in writing or oral. If the Public Guardian or a Visitor is providing a report required by the Court of Protection then they may examine and take copies of Health and Social Services records. They may also interview the person in private. A Court of Protection Special Visitor may if the court so directs carry out in private a medical, psychiatric or psychological examination of the person's capacity and condition (s 49(9)).

When might an application be made?

Most acts in connection with the care or treatment of a person lacking capacity can lawfully be performed under s 5, subject to the restrictions and limitations imposed by s 6 (see Chapter 7) and there will be no need to make an application to the Court of Protection. In particular it would be inappropriate to apply to the court where the situation was clear but the health or social care professional simply wanted the security of the court's sanction. The following are some examples of where an application might be appropriate:

- where the cumulative restrictions or restraints imposed upon a person who lacked capacity amounted to a deprivation of liberty and therefore could not lawfully be imposed as a s 5 act;

- where the court has determined that certain categories of decisions in respect of people who lacked capacity required an application (for example, withdrawing artificial nutrition and hydration from a patient in a persistent vegetative state);

- where there were genuine concerns about the manner in which an attorney or a deputy was acting (for example, apparently ignoring the best interests checklist);

- where there was doubt over the meaning or construction of an LPA or whether an advance decision was valid or applicable;

- where it was felt that there might be a need for a deputy to be appointed;

- where an existing receiver under an EPA wished to have clarification or an extension of his powers;

- where despite following the statutory provisions and the guidance contained in the Code of Practice a decision-maker found it impossible to decide either whether the person lacked capacity in relation to a matter or, if he lacked capacity, whether what was proposed was in his best interests;

- where a provision in the Act was unclear and needed interpretation (for example, whether a particular form of treatment constituted life-sustaining treatment);

- where a person wished to challenge a determination that he lacked capacity in relation to a matter;

- where an IMCA believed that a decision-maker was failing to take into account his submissions as to what was in the best interests of a person lacking capacity.

This is not intended to be an exhaustive list but rather one designed to illustrate the broad range of decisions and declarations that the Court of Protection has power to make if requested. If in doubt about whether a court decision is needed the Office of Public Guardian should be approached for advice (see below, page 74).

Who can apply to the Court of Protection?

From the above list of circumstances in which an application to the Court of Protection might be considered, it can be seen that the application itself could come from an NHS Trust, a local authority, an allegedly incapacitated person, or from somebody wanting to be able to deal with the money and property of a person lacking capacity.

Comprehensive rules have been issued (Court of Protection Rules 2007 No. 1744) which govern the practice and procedure of the Court of Protection. Section 50(1) sets out a list of those people who do not need to have prior permission before applying to the Court of Protection, and these have been extended by rule 51 as follows:

- a person who lacks or allegedly lacks capacity (and if under 18 anyone with parental responsibility for him);

- the donor or donee (attorney) of an LPA to which the application relates;

- a deputy appointed by the court for a person to whom the application relates;

- a person named in an existing order of the court if the application relates to that order;

- the Official Solicitor or the Public Guardian;

- anyone, if the application concerns an LPA purportedly created under the Act;

- anyone, if the application concerns an EPA within the meaning of Schedule 4 to the Act;

- anyone, if (with certain exceptions set out in rule 52) the application relates solely to the exercise of the court's powers in relation to a person's property and affairs.

In any other circumstances (apart from declarations as to private international law) permission is required to make an application to the Court of Protection. In deciding whether to grant permission the court must in particular have regard to:

- the applicant's connection with the person to whom the application relates;

- the reasons for the application;

- the benefit to a person to whom the application relates of a proposed order or directions; and

- whether the benefit can be achieved in any other way.

The Procedural Rules also include: when hearings can be dispensed with (rule 84), when the hearing may be held in private, the form in which evidence is to be given (Part 14) and orders for costs (rules 156–7). The general rule in respect of costs is that the court will not order one party to pay the costs of another and can order in appropriate circumstances that costs are paid out of the estate of the person lacking capacity. Permission to appeal will normally be required (except from an order for committal) and if the original order was made by a district judge appeal will be to a circuit judge; if from a circuit judge then to a High Court judge and thence to the Court of Appeal with permission.

The Code of Practice deals with the availability of public funding at 15.38–44. The fees for application to the Court of Protection and for the services provided by the Public Guardian are set out respectively in the Court of Protection Fees Order 2007 No. 1745, and the Public Guardian (Fees, etc.) Regulations 2007 No. 2051.

Court of Protection Visitors

Court of Protection Visitors are appointed by the Lord Chancellor. There are two panels: a panel of Special Visitors and a panel of General Visitors. Special Visitors must be either registered medical practitioners or appear to the Lord Chancellor to have other suitable qualifications or training and to have special knowledge of and experience in cases of impairment of or disturbance in the functioning of the mind or brain. They may be requested either by the court or by the Public Guardian to visit and make reports on people who lack capacity. They may interview the person in private and have a right to see and take copies of relevant health and social care records. Special Visitors may if directed by the court carry out in private a medical, psychiatric or psychological examination of the person's capacity and condition. The Code of Practice at 14.10–11 highlights the Visitors' role in also interviewing attorneys or deputies and supporting them in carrying out their duties. General Visitors could come from a range of backgrounds and report to the court on issues such as whether attorneys are acting within their legal remit as well as in a person's best interests.

The Public Guardian

Section 57 creates a new public official known as the Public Guardian, appointed by the Lord Chancellor. The Public Guardian is overseen by a Public Guardian Board established under s 59 whose function is to scrutinise and review the way in which the Public Guardian discharges his functions and to make recommendations to the Lord Chancellor. The Board Regulations have now been issued and the first Public Guardian has been appointed. The Public Guardian's website is at **www.guardianship.gov.uk**. The functions of the Public Guardian are set out in s 58 and include the following:

- establishing and maintaining registers of LPAs and court-appointed deputies;

- supervising deputies;

- directing Court of Protection Visitors to visit and report to him on LPA attorneys, deputies, or the person lacking capacity;

- receiving reports from deputies or attorneys;

- providing reports to the Court of Protection as directed under s 49(2);

- dealing with representations and complaints about the way in which attorneys or deputies are exercising their powers.

In carrying out his functions under the second and last of the above, the Public Guardian is empowered to work co-operatively with other people who have responsibilities for the care or treatment of persons lacking capacity.

The Public Guardian's functions are expanded upon in the Lasting Powers of Attorney, Enduring Powers of Attorney and Public Guardian Regulations, in particular in relation to requiring security or the manner in which information is sought from attorneys under LPAs and EPAs.

How will the Public Guardian operate in practice?

From comments made on behalf of the Government and by the Public Guardian, it was clearly anticipated that the role of the Public Guardian should not be confined to the formal exercise of his powers and functions. So in the Department of Constitutional Affairs' overview of the original Mental Incapacity Bill it was stated that the Public Guardian:

> *will also offer advice to the public on matters to do with adults who lack capacity . . . we envisage that the Public Guardian will work with other organisations involved in the care and well-being of adults who lack capacity in order to provide a complete approach to problems and possible abuse. The Public Guardian will also work with attorneys and deputies who may need help and support in carrying out their duties.*

No doubt mindful of the restriction on the availability of public funding for applications to the Court of Protection and in relation to the Act generally (there is specialist limited publicly funded legal advice available where necessary for cases of particular seriousness and complexity), the Government envisages that the Public Guardian will offer a telephone information line. In an early statement the Public Guardian stated:

> *Working in effective partnership with the judiciary it will be our role to ensure that appropriate supervision regimes are in place which balance the autonomy of the individual with the most appropriate protection against abuse. We are currently considering how this regime can be effective yet as unobtrusive as possible. We will also have a role in providing the public with information about mental capacity issues and signposting people to the most appropriate form of help and assistance.*

This emphasis on the broader constructive role that the Public Guardian will play is highlighted in the Code of Practice. So along with the responsibility for maintaining the registers, checking documentation before registration, and investigating allegations of abuse by attorneys and deputies, the focus is on:

- providing information to help potential donors understand the impact of making an LPA, what they can give an attorney authority to do, and what to consider when choosing an attorney (14.12);

- supporting deputies in carrying out their duties (14.15);

- working co-operatively with local authorities and NHS Trusts (14.14;14.20);

- running checks on potential deputies including risk assessments 'to determine what supervision a deputy will need once they are appointed' (14.17);

- being available to 'anybody who is caring for a person who lacks capacity, whether in a paid or unpaid role, who is worried about how attorneys or deputies carry out their duties' (14.19);

- being approached for guidance and advice in relation to disagreements about the finances of a person lacking capacity (15.34);

- referring concerns about personal welfare LPAs or personal welfare deputies to the relevant agency including, in certain circumstances, the police (14.21).

As gatekeeper to the Court of Protection one can expect the Public Guardian when approached to recommend alternative methods of resolving disputes falling short of a formal application to the court, such as mediation, as well as to recognise those more complex issues which require a court decision. In theory the Office of the Public Guardian could be a useful and constructive source of information and advice to anyone faced with making difficult judgments in respect of a person lacking capacity. Whether the suggestions to this effect, which were made in the run-up to the Act coming into force, in fact materialise remains to be seen.

Multiple choice questions

Read each question carefully and tick the appropriate box(es). Where a statement is correct, tick the box next to it; if it is incorrect, leave it blank. You may need to tick more than one box per question.

Appendix 5 (pages 145–9) gives the answers.

12.1 *The following would be typical situations where the Court of Protection would be involved:*

 (a) *it was felt that there might be the need for a deputy to be appointed* ☐

 (b) *a person was appealing against detention under the Mental Health Act* ☐

 (c) *a person wished to challenge a decision that he lacked capacity in relation to a matter* ☐

 (d) *a nearest relative wanted to make an application for guardianship* ☐

 (e) *someone alleged that an attorney was not applying the best interests checklist* ☐

 (f) *an IMCA believed a decision-maker was failing to take into account his submissions as to what was in the best interests of a person lacking capacity* ☐

12.2 *The Court of Protection can only intervene if the person in question has a mental disorder as defined by the Mental Health Act 1983:*

 (a) *True* ☐

 (b) *False* ☐

12.3 *The Public Guardian is responsible for:*

 (a) *establishing and maintaining registers of LPAs* ☐

 (b) *establishing and maintaining registers of guardianships under the Mental Health Act* ☐

 (c) *supervising court-appointed deputies* ☐

 (d) *supervising nearest relatives appointed by the County Court* ☐

 (e) *directing Court of Protection Visitors to visit and report on persons lacking capacity* ☐

 (f) *receiving reports from deputies or attorneys* ☐

Chapter 13
Other issues

Ill-treatment and neglect (section 44)

A new criminal offence of ill-treatment or neglect is created by s 44. Whilst not a central part of the scheme of the Act it is one of a number of protective mechanisms and safeguards reinforcing other measures such as Adult Protection Committees. The section does not create a single offence but rather separate offences of ill-treatment or neglect, carrying a maximum sentence of five years' imprisonment. Based on earlier court decisions ill-treatment must be either deliberately or recklessly undertaken, whether or not actual harm was caused. 'Wilful neglect' is not defined but the Code of Practice states that it usually means that a person has deliberately failed to carry out an act they knew they had a duty to do.

The offence can be committed by:

- a person having care of someone who lacks or whom he reasonably believes to lack capacity;

- a person appointed under a Lasting Power of Attorney or an Enduring Power of Attorney created by the victim;

- a deputy appointed by the Court of Protection for the victim.

The victim may be under the age of 16. This is one of the rare occasions when the Act does not apply just to those over the age of 16 (see Chapter 15).

No further definition is given of a person who lacks capacity. It is possible that this will create difficulties in practice given the scheme of the Act, which emphasises the time- and decision-specific nature of capacity; in other words the Act and Code of Practice strongly discourage unqualified assertions of lack of capacity, requiring the functional test to be applied to the specific circumstances in which the person finds himself. The question is not 'does this person lack capacity?' but rather 'in relation to *what* does he lack capacity?' What is the act in respect of which the person must lack capacity in order for him to constitute a potential victim of this offence? Is it whether he has capacity to make a decision to protect himself, or to make other kinds of decisions, and if so which? It is both curious and unfortunate that the concept of lack of capacity is neither defined nor qualified in this context.

Exclusions

Chapter 15 examines the interface between the Mental Capacity Act and the Mental Health Act, in particular the provisions of s 28 relating to someone detained under the

Mental Health Act whose treatment is regulated under Part 4. The non-applicability of the Mental Capacity Act in relation to such patients is strictly limited and so does not cover for example the issue of consenting to *admission* to hospital but only to treatment covered by Part 4. In many circumstances the Mental Capacity Act will apply in relation to a patient formally detained under the Mental Health Act, for example when treatment for a physical condition rather than for mental disorder is in issue. It will also apply of course to informal patients. The definition of incapacity in s 2(1) is qualified by the words 'for the purposes of this Act', and the standard of proof set out in s 2(4) by the words 'in proceedings under this Act or any other enactment'; Schedule 6 makes a number of amendments to other Acts to make their interpretation of incapacity consistent with the Act but does not affect the test for insanity or fitness to plead to a criminal charge; the Code of Practice refers (4.32) to the continued applicability of other tests of capacity in different contexts such as capacity to make a will. While this may be strictly true, if the functional test is applied, and the specific decision placed in context, the use of the Act's test of incapacity in such other contexts is unlikely to result in a different outcome. What is more likely to differ is the identity of the decision-maker, the person who will make the assessment of capacity. Thus in practice the definition and test for incapacity set out in the Act are likely to be used ever more widely in future.

Specific exclusions

Section 27 sets out certain specifically excluded decisions, which cannot be made on behalf of a person lacking capacity. Section 27 precludes:

- consenting to marriage or a civil partnership;

- consenting to sexual relations;

- consenting to a decree of divorce or the dissolution of a civil partnership on the basis of two years' separation;

- consenting to a child being placed for adoption or to the making of an adoption order;

- discharging parental responsibilities in matters not relating to a child's property;

- giving consent under the Human Fertilisation and Embryology Act 1990.

Section 29 precludes voting at an election or at a referendum on behalf of a person lacking capacity.

Section 62 provides that for the avoidance of doubt nothing in the Act is to be taken to affect the law relating to murder, manslaughter or assisting suicide. This declaratory provision is strictly speaking unnecessary and was inserted to give reassurance to those who argued or who were concerned that the provisions in particular relating to personal welfare LPAs and advance decisions constituted a slippery slope leading towards euthanasia.

Finally, it needs to be remembered that s 2(5) provides that the powers exercisable under the Act in relation to a person lacking or reasonably thought to lack capacity are not exercisable in relation to a person under 16; it is subject to the power of the Court of

Protection under s 18(3) to make an order in respect of a person's property and affairs even though he is under the age of 16 if it considers it likely that he will still lack capacity to make decisions in respect of that matter when he reaches 18; this does not include the making of a statutory will. Remember also that a person under the age of 18 may not make an advance decision, or execute an LPA or be appointed an attorney.

Chapter 14
Research

Introduction

Sections 30–34 of the Mental Capacity Act, together with associated Regulations, provide a comprehensive set of safeguards in relation to research projects involving a person who lacks capacity. Research is not defined in the Act but includes direct medical interventions and also covers asking patients' views about health and social care services, observing them in a social care setting and research on medical notes (where not anonymised).

What research is affected by the Act?

Section 30 provides that 'intrusive research' carried out on or in relation to a person who lacks capacity is unlawful unless it is part of an approved research project and complies with the provisions relating to consultation and other safeguards contained in ss 32 and 33. 'Intrusive research' means research which would be unlawful unless, where consent was required, the research subject had capacity to consent to his involvement and did consent. A research project must be approved by an appropriate body which Regulations define as a recognised Research Ethics Committee.

The Act does not apply to clinical trials which are subject to the provisions of the Medicines for Human Use (Clinical Trials) Regulations 2004, because these regulations already provide for participants who lack capacity. Because of the way intrusive research is defined the Act will not cover research not requiring the consent of a participant. So research on anonymised medical data or (provided Research Ethics Committee approval has been obtained) on anonymised human tissue is not included.

It is also possible to obtain approval under s 251 of the NHS Act 2006 to use confidential patient information without the patient's consent. Although the Act does not repeat the requirements of the Human Tissue Act 2004 in relation to the storage or use of tissue, for example for transplants and research, the relevant provisions so far as they concern adults lacking capacity are covered in the Code of Practice at chapter 11.37–40.

The requirements for approval

Before approval can be given for a research project s 31 sets out a number of pre-qualifying conditions.

- The research must be connected with an 'impairing condition' or its treatment. 'Impairing condition' means one that is or may be attributable to or causes or contributes to the impairment of or disturbance in the functioning of the person's mind or brain. As the Explanatory Notes to the Act set out this limits the sort of research projects that the person may be involved in but will include research into the effects of the impairment on his health and day-to-day life as well as into the causes or possible causes of the impairment and its treatment.

- There must be reasonable grounds for believing that research of comparable effectiveness cannot be carried out if it has to be confined to people who have capacity to consent.

- The research must *either* (1) have the potential to benefit the person lacking capacity without imposing on him a burden disproportionate to the potential benefit to him *or* (2) be intended to provide knowledge of the causes or treatment of or of the care of persons affected by the same or a similar condition. If relying on (2) above there must be reasonable grounds for believing that the risk to the person lacking capacity is negligible and does not constitute a significant interference with his privacy or freedom or be unduly invasive or restrictive. In addition he must be withdrawn from the project if the researcher believes at any time that these conditions no longer apply, unless to do so would pose a significant risk to his health (s 33(5)). At Chapter 11.14 the Code of Practice gives examples of potential benefits of research for a person who lacks capacity. These could be: developing more effective ways of treating a person or managing his condition; improving the quality of health care, social care or other services to which he has access; discovering the cause of his condition; or reducing the risk of his being harmed, excluded or disadvantaged.

The requirement of consultation

The consultation requirements of the Act are set out in s 32. Before enrolling a person into an approved research project the researcher must take reasonable steps to identify someone with whom he can consult; this must not be somebody professionally involved with the care of that person nor a paid carer but someone interested in his welfare and who is prepared to be consulted. An attorney appointed under an LPA or a deputy appointed by the court could fulfil this role.

If the researcher is unable to identify such a person he must nominate somebody unconnected with the research project but willing to be consulted. Guidance to be followed in respect of this process has been issued (in draft form).

Once the consultee has been identified he or she must be provided with relevant information about the project and asked whether the person lacking capacity should take part and what he or she thinks that person would have said if he had capacity. If the consultee advises that the person would not have wished to take part in the research project the researcher must ensure that he does not participate; if he is already participating he must be withdrawn from it unless the researcher believes on reasonable grounds that to do so would pose a significant risk to the person's health.

If the person lacking capacity is having or is about to have urgent treatment and the researcher believes that it is necessary for him to take urgent action for the purposes of the research and that it is impracticable to follow the consultation requirements, he can proceed (for so long as it remains urgent) if he obtains the agreement of a doctor (unconnected with the research project) or, where there is no time, he follows a procedure covering such an eventuality which will have been approved in advance by the Research Ethics Committee. As the Code of Practice points out (11.36) this exception to the duty to consult is likely to be limited to research into procedures or treatments used in emergencies. The Explanatory Notes give as an example a paramedic or doctor making measurements in the first few minutes following a serious head injury or stroke. The exception does not apply where the researcher simply wants to act quickly.

Other safeguards

Section 33 imposes further limits on what can be done to a person lacking capacity who has been enrolled in an approved research project. The researcher cannot do anything to which the person appears to object unless it is necessary to do so to protect him from harm or reduce pain or discomfort suffered by him. In addition the researcher must withdraw the person without delay from the project if he indicates in any way that he wishes to be withdrawn. If the person has made a valid and applicable advance decision or any other form of statement refusing consent to anything being done or proposed to be done to him during the research project the researcher may not proceed. There is a presumption in favour of the interests of the person lacking capacity outweighing those of science and society.

Section 34 deals with the situation where a person loses capacity during a research project begun before s 30 was in force and provides that Regulations may be made permitting the person's continued involvement in accordance with the requirements of the Regulations which may include provisions similar to those contained in ss 31–33. The Regulations have been issued as the Mental Capacity Act 2005 Loss of Capacity during Research Project (England) Regulations 2007 No. 679 and do indeed contain such provisions.

Chapter 15
Links with other areas of law

Links with the Human Rights Act 1998

The relationship between the Mental Capacity Act and the Human Rights Act is a crucial one for practitioners. This chapter will begin with an outline of the key provisions and then explore some of the issues linking the two pieces of legislation. The Human Rights Act 1998 became operational in October 2000. It does not incorporate the whole of the European Convention on Human Rights but it does include the following Articles which are relevant in varying degrees in the field of mental capacity:

Article 2 **Right to life.** Everyone's right to life shall be protected by law.

Article 3 **Prohibition of torture.** No one to be subject to torture or inhuman or degrading treatment or punishment. *This has a fairly high threshold but might be breached by excessive use of control and restraint.*

Article 4 **Prohibition of slavery and forced labour**

Article 5 **Right to liberty and security of person.** 5.1 No one shall be deprived of their liberty except for specific cases and in accordance with procedure pre-scribed by law . . . e.g. after conviction, lawful arrest on suspicion of having committed an offence, lawful detention of person of unsound mind, to pre-vent spread of infectious diseases. 5.4 Everyone deprived of liberty by arrest or detention shall be entitled to take proceedings by which the lawfulness of the detention shall be decided speedily by a Court and release ordered if the detention is not lawful.

Note that in the *Bournewood* case (*HL v UK*) which is discussed below, the European Court ruled that there had been breaches of Article 5.1 and 5.4.

Article 6 **Right to a fair trial.** Everyone is entitled to a fair and public hearing within a reasonable time by an independent and impartial Tribunal.

Article 7 **No punishment without law**

Article 8 **Right to respect for private and family life** Everyone has the right to respect for his private and family life, his home and his correspondence.

Article 9 **Freedom of thought, conscience and religion**

Article 10   Freedom of expression

Article 11   Freedom of assembly and association

Article 12   **Right to marry.** Men and women of marriageable age have the right to marry and to found a family. *This is largely outside the remit of the Mental Capacity Act because of the exclusions in s 27.*

Article 14   **Prohibition of discrimination** Enjoyment of the rights and freedoms set forth in this Convention shall be secured without discrimination on any ground such as sex, race, colour, language, religion, political or other opinion, national or social origin, association with a national minority, property, birth or other status.

Relevance of the Human Rights Act 1998 in the passage of the Bill

It is not surprising that the Parliamentary Joint Committee on Human Rights concentrated so heavily in its deliberations, reports and questioning of Government about the Mental Incapacity Bill on the question of potential breaches of Article 5 of the European Convention (Council of Europe, 1950). These largely took place in the aftermath of the European Court decision in *HL v UK* when in the context of the Bill concerns surrounding deprivation of liberty, its extent and process were very much to the fore. The concern that the Bill permitted involuntary placement of incapacitated people on the authority of s 5, and the absence of any proposals to fill the 'Bournewood gap' preoccupied the committee.

The Government's eventual response was, in relation to the first issue, to prohibit the use of s 5 to deprive an incapacitated person of liberty, and, in relation to the second issue, to produce in the Mental Health Bill (now Mental Health Act 2007) its proposals for a new procedure prescribed by law to authorise deprivations of liberty. Both these responses create problems of their own. If an incapacitated person could not lawfully be deprived of his liberty under s 5 this raised the difficulty of what lawful avenues were open to care for people in such circumstances, certainly until the advent of the new Court of Protection in October 2007. The 'Bournewood gap' provisions are unlikely to take effect until April 2009, leaving health and social care professionals with a period of uncertainty as to whether they are providing care in circumstances amounting to an unauthorised deprivation of liberty. These issues are covered in detail in Chapter 16.

Elsewhere within the Act there is potential for breaches of Articles 2, 3, 6, 8 and 14. The role, powers of and access to the new Court of Protection are likely to ensure that the Act is compliant with the Article 6 right to a fair trial, which covers not merely criminal proceedings but all proceedings where an individual's civil rights are in issue. Whether the 'Bournewood gap' proposals are sufficiently compliant with Article 6 remains to be seen. The principle of equal consideration, namely that a determination as to a person's best interests must not be made merely on the basis of the person's age or appearance, or a condition of his, or an aspect of his behaviour, which might lead others to make unjustified assumptions about what might be in his best interests, coupled with the presumption of capacity goes a long way towards ensuring that the Act complies with the Article 14 prohibition against discrimination of an individual's enjoyment of rights and freedoms guaranteed by the Convention.

This leaves for more detailed consideration of Article 2 (the right to life), Article 3 (the prohibition against torture or inhuman and degrading treatment or punishment), and Article 8 (the right to respect for private and family life).

Articles 2, 3, and 8 of the European Convention on Human Rights

It might be thought that an Act which has, as one of its principal objectives, the active promotion of the rights of people lacking capacity (both in the process of assessing their capacity to make decisions, and in the way that decisions are made in their best interests when they lack capacity) would be unlikely to come into conflict with provisions of the European Convention. Indeed the scheme for personal welfare Lasting Powers of Attorneys is compatible with the Convention because the attorney is chosen by a person who must have capacity to make the appointment and understand its implications. In addition the attorney is governed by the best interests checklist and by guidance contained within the Code of Practice and is ultimately accountable for his actions to the Court of Protection.

Even around the question of withholding or withdrawing consent to life-sustaining treatment the human rights issues arise from consideration of the adequacy of the safeguards rather than from the principle itself. Advance decisions to refuse treatment have been an accepted part of the common law for many years. It is generally accepted that the requirement to give life-sustaining treatment in the face of a valid and applicable advance refusal (which might be argued as implicit in Article 2 as a result of the positive nature of the obligation of the state to secure Convention rights for its citizens) gives way to the Article 8 right of a competent person to medical autonomy and indeed in appropriate cases to the Article 3 prohibition against inhuman and degrading treatment.

On the other hand the possibility of abuse or misunderstanding has to be considered. So, in codifying and clarifying the common law principle on which advance decisions are based, a number of safeguards are provided – the requirement that an advance decision be valid and applicable, and spelling out circumstances in which it is not. The formal requirements where an advance decision is made to refuse life-sustaining treatment go beyond the previous requirements of the common law. The fact that a doctor is free to treat unless he is satisfied that there is a valid and applicable advance decision in existence (s 26(2)), dealt with in Chapter 10, is a considerable safeguard, resolving doubts in favour of the presumption of preserving life.

Is there a requirement to go further? The Joint Committee urged the Government to introduce a requirement that *all* advance decisions be in writing to reduce possible misunderstanding, but there seems no logical reason why a person who has capacity should not be able simply in conversation with, for example, a healthcare professional to declare his refusal of specific treatment without being required to put it in writing. The healthcare professional may well decide to make a careful note as a sensible safeguard but given the presumption referred to above and the requirement to be satisfied as to the validity and applicability of an advance decision, to go further appears unnecessary, particularly when set against the declared aim of empowering people to make more decisions for themselves when they have the capacity to do so. It may add to the difficulties for a healthcare professional in deciding whether a verbal advance decision is valid or applicable but that is insufficient reason to add such a formal requirement. Overall the additional safeguards and clarifications provided in the Act compared to the vagueness of the common law position make it very unlikely that the framework for advance decisions will lead to breaches of Article 2 or 3.

The Joint Committee had a particular concern in respect of decisions to withdraw artificial nutrition and hydration (ANH). This was because they feared that the decision in *Airedale NHS Trust v Bland* that giving artificial nutrition and hydration constituted medical treatment which could therefore in appropriate circumstances lawfully be withdrawn by healthcare professionals was not widely understood by the general public. The committee was concerned that in making advance decisions covering refusal of life-sustaining treatment, or in appointing a personal welfare attorney with power to consent to or refuse life-sustaining treatment, it would not be appreciated that this would cover ANH. The Government declined to amend the definition of life-sustaining treatment in the Act to include specific reference to ANH but did agree that the Code of Practice should make the position clear, which it does at Chapter 9.26. This seems sufficient in the circumstances.

Where there is no valid and applicable advance decision in existence it must be remembered that in appointing a personal welfare deputy the Court of Protection cannot give him power to refuse consent to the carrying out or continuation of life-sustaining treatment (s 20(5)). Further for a personal welfare LPA covering consent to medical treatment, if this is intended to include consent to or refusal of life-sustaining treatment that must be explicitly stated. In addition the prescribed information contained in the form for creating a personal welfare LPA contains an explanation of life-sustaining treatment. These provisions, together with s 62 which declares for the avoidance of doubt that nothing in the Act is to be taken to affect the law relating to murder or manslaughter or assisted suicide, almost certainly provide sufficient safeguards to satisfy the positive obligation of the state to protect life.

A similar issue regarding the adequacy of safeguards concerned the Joint Committee in relation to research involving people lacking capacity, drawing unfavourable comparisons with the stringent requirements of the Convention on Human Rights and Biomedicine as to the nature of the benefit of the research to the person lacking capacity or others with the same or similar conditions, the nature of the risk of harm, and the meaning and effect of the 'no alternative' criterion (i.e. that the research could not equally well be carried out on individuals able to consent). This seems a little harsh, given the welter of safeguards relating to the initial approval of the project, the requirement of consultation, the provision for participants losing capacity part way through the project (see Chapter 14), and it is unlikely that if the requirements of the Act and Regulations are followed there will be any breach of the participant's Article 2 or 3 rights, and any breach of his Article 8 rights is likely to be justified under Article 8(2).

Links with the Mental Health Act 1983

There are several areas where working within the remit of the Mental Capacity Act is likely to bring people into contact with the Mental Health Act. These are:

(i) informal admissions to psychiatric hospitals of those who lack capacity to make a decision about admission;

(ii) treatment within psychiatric hospital of those who lack capacity to give valid consent to the treatment in question;

(iii) decisions on matters that fall outside the remit of the Mental Health Act for those who are subject to compulsion within its provisions;

(iv) decisions on matters that fall within the remit of the Mental Health Act but where someone has been appointed as a deputy or where a Lasting Power of Attorney exists.

A key issue will be whenever a person's circumstances amount to a deprivation of liberty rather than restriction of movement as there are serious limitations on what can be dealt with under the Mental Capacity Act in these circumstances. This will be considered once we have addressed the question of who can come within the remit of the Mental Heath Act. This is not just a question which occurs when a person is detained, as the definition of mental disorder also applies to informal patients, whether they are in effect 'voluntary' or lacking capacity to make a decision on admission and are in hospital in their best interests.

Mental incapacity compared with mental disorder

It is important to avoid assumptions that people who have a mental disorder will lack the capacity to make decisions about health and social matters. It is also important not to assume that a lack of capacity to make a particular decision must be caused by a mental disorder. This, however, is a little more difficult to assert when the definition of mental disorder is so broad, and becoming broader. At one point in the Government's moves to reform mental health law, the definition of mental disorder was almost identical to that of mental incapacity, as it was then described in the Mental Incapacity Bill. If this had remained the case there would potentially have been even more problems with people muddling up the two concepts.

Starting with the first assertion, that people who have a mental disorder will not automatically lack the capacity to make decisions about health and social matters, this should be clear as soon as an individual situation is looked at. Even if a mental disorder, say severe depression, affects capacity in some areas of a person's decision-making it is unlikely to rob the individual of all decision-making powers. Even in cases of severe depression, dementia or severe learning difficulties there will be some decisions that the individual will be able to make. The definition of mental incapacity in the Mental Capacity Act starts with the phrase 'unable to make a decision for himself in relation to the matter' which should help clarify the issue. No-one should have the general label 'mentally incapacitated' attached to them; 'mental incapacity' only has meaning in relation to a specific issue.

The second assertion, that there are causes of incapacity which are other than mental disorder, is usually accepted but note that the current definition of mental disorder in the Mental Health Act 1983 includes 'any other disorder or disability of mind' as well as mental illness, arrested or incomplete development of mind and psychopathic disorder. Quite what amounts to any 'disorder or disability of mind' will become even more of a focus of attention when the 2007 Mental Health Act is implemented as it will then be the only definition of mental disorder, with the other categories and most of the exclusions being dropped. It is not clear as to which 'impairments or disturbances in the functioning of the mind or brain' (the phrase used in the Mental Capacity Act but which does not appear in the Mental Health Act) will *not* amount to mental disorder.

When the 'Bournewood' safeguards are implemented (probably in April 2009) this will become an issue in many cases, as there will be a 'mental disorder' test before the new provisions can be used. Areas of controversy will probably include: strokes, physical illnesses which can affect thinking (e.g. diabetes), and the long-term effects of drugs or alcohol. For other areas of the Mental Capacity Act where there may be requests for immediate interventions, there would, again, be issues associated with the effects of drugs or alcohol as well as situations such as concussion following a head injury. These impairments are not usually seen as 'mental disorders' for the purposes of the Mental Health Act although they are 'impairments or disturbances in the functioning of the mind or brain'. It will be interesting to see how custom and practice, and/or case, law develop in this area. It is not an area of idle speculation, as important matters such as funding can hang on such decisions.

Deprivation of liberty

As noted above in the discussion on the Human Rights Act, this issue was addressed in the *Bournewood* case. There were various stages to this case and those who wish to pursue its history in more depth may wish to consult the *Approved Social Worker's Guide to Mental Health Law* (Brown, 2006). In order to understand the links with the Mental Capacity Act we need to look just at the most recent decision which was a European Court judgment. In particular we need to consider the implications of the ruling on the question of what amounts to 'deprivation of liberty' as opposed to mere 'restriction of movement'. The following summary of the case is taken from the European Judgment of *HL v UK* (2005).

> *The applicant was born in 1949 and he lives in Surrey. He has suffered from autism since birth. He is unable to speak and his level of understanding is limited. He is frequently agitated and has a history of self-harming behaviour. He lacks the capacity to consent or object to medical treatment. For over 30 years he was cared for in Bournewood Hospital . . . He was an in-patient at the Intensive Behavioural Unit (IBU) of the hospital from its inception in or around 1987. The applicant's responsible medical officer (who had cared for him since 1977) was Dr M . . . In March 1994 he was discharged on a trial basis to paid carers, Mr and Mrs E, with whom he successfully resided until 22 July 1997. . . [He] was at the day centre when he became particularly agitated, hitting himself on the head with his fists and banging his head against the wall. Staff could not contact Mr and Mrs E and got in touch with a local doctor who*

administered a sedative. The applicant remained agitated and on the recommendation of the local authority care services manager (AF) with overall responsibility for the applicant, the applicant was taken to the accident and emergency unit at the hospital. At the hospital, the applicant remained agitated and anxious and was received and assessed by Dr P (Acting Consultant Psychiatrist – Learning Disabilities Services) as being in need of in-patient treatment. The applicant was transferred, with the physical support of two nursing assistants, to the IBU of the hospital. He was recorded as making no attempt to leave. Having consulted, Dr P and Dr M considered that the best interests of the applicant required his admission for in-patient treatment. Dr M did consider his committal under the Mental Health Act 1983 ('the 1983 Act') but concluded that that was not necessary as the applicant was compliant and did not resist admission. The applicant was therefore admitted as an 'informal patient'. Dr M later confirmed (in her submissions in the judicial review proceedings referred to below) that if the applicant had resisted admission, she would have detained him compulsorily under the 1983 Act as she was firmly of the view that he required in-patient treatment.

The carers were discouraged from visiting at this point. In a report on 18 August Dr M concluded that HL suffered from a mood disorder as well as autism and that his discharge would be against medical opinion. In the first instance the carers sought a writ of habeas corpus from the High Court in the hope that HL would be released into their care. This failed but on 29 October 1997 the Court of Appeal indicated it would decide the appeal in the applicant's favour. HL was then held on s 5(2) and on 31 October an application for s 3 under the Mental Health Act 1983 was made. On 2 November he was seen by his carers for the first time since July. Application was made to the MHRT in November and independent psychiatric reports were obtained recommending HL's discharge. Before a MHRT hearing, application was also made for a Managers' Hearing. On 5 December 1997 HL was allowed home on s 17 leave and on 12 December the Managers discharged him from the s 3. The case, however, continued its journey through the courts. After the Law Lords had overturned the Court of Appeal judgment the case was eventually heard in the European Court where it was decided that HL had indeed been deprived of his liberty whilst an 'informal' patient and that this was in breach of Article 5 of the European Convention on Human Rights which states:

No one shall be deprived of their liberty except for specific cases and in accordance with procedure prescribed by law e.g. after conviction, lawful arrest on suspicion of having committed an offence, lawful detention of person of unsound mind, to prevent spread of infectious diseases. Everyone deprived of liberty by arrest or detention shall be entitled to take proceedings by which the lawfulness of the detention shall be decided speedily by a Court and release ordered if the detention is not lawful.

The court considered that the key factor in the case was that the healthcare professionals treating and managing the applicant had exercised *complete and effective control* over his care and movements from the moment he presented acute behavioural problems to the date he was compulsorily detained, a period of three months. He was only going to be released from the hospital to the care of Mr and Mrs E when those professionals considered it appropriate. *HL was under continuous supervision and control and was not free to leave.* It was not crucial that the door to the ward was locked or lockable.

The court accepted that HL was suffering from a mental disorder of a kind or degree warranting compulsory confinement. However, the court found that there had been a breach of Article 5.1 in that there was an absence of procedural safeguards to protect against arbitrary deprivation of liberty in the reliance on the common law doctrine of necessity. Article 5.4 was also breached in that the applicant had no right to have the lawfulness of his detention reviewed speedily by a court. Judicial review and habeas corpus proceedings were not adequate. Although other Articles of the ECHR were clearly relevant (e.g. Article 8, the right to respect for private and family life) the court only ruled on Articles 5.1 and 5.4.

Procedural safeguards for those detained under the Mental Health Act 1983

The European Court noted that the following safeguards would apply as soon as a person was detained under the Mental Health Act:

(a) Statutory criteria needed to be met and applied by two doctors and an applicant;

(b) Part IV consent to treatment procedures;

(c) Applications and automatic referrals to MH Review Tribunals;

(d) Nearest relative powers (including discharge powers);

(e) Section 117 after-care;

(f) The Code of Practice and the Mental Health Act Commission;

(g) Section 132 rights to information.

Implications of the Bournewood case

Each case will need to be looked at on its own merits but in a situation similar to that of HL it would not be safe to rely on the Mental Capacity Act to justify deprivation of liberty, especially where the criteria for detention under the Mental Health Act appear to be met. In such circumstances the Mental Health Act should be used. If the criteria for detention under the Mental Health Act are not met, then an application to the Court of Protection should be considered.

In a more recent case (*JE v DE (1), Surrey CC (2)*, 2006) a High Court judge also used the phrase 'not free to leave' when he ruled that a man who had been kept against his will in a residential care home, rather than at home with his wife, had been deprived of his liberty. There had been no use of guardianship to justify the position and no declaration had been sought from the High Court by the local authority.

The equivalent from October 2007 would have been for the decision-maker (an officer of the local authority in these circumstances) to have applied to the Court of Protection, as the level of restraint went beyond restriction of movement. Alternatively the use of the Mental Health Act could have been pursued.

The plans to fill the 'Bournewood gap' are outlined in Chapter 16. Until these proposals are enacted staff are encouraged by the Department of Health (2004) guidance to try and care for people in a way that falls short of depriving them of their liberty. However, if this is not possible, the guidance states at paragraph 32:

> *Until these safeguards are established in law, the effect of the judgment is that it would be unlawful for an NHS body or a local authority (without the prior authorisation of the High Court) to arrange or provide care or treatment for an incapacitated patient in a way that amounted to deprivation of liberty within the meaning of article 5 of the Convention, unless the patient were detained under the Mental Health Act 1983.*

The proposals go beyond the situation of HL (who was a 'compliant' patient in a hospital) to cover the circumstances of the thousands of people who are resident in nursing or care homes where the only options at present are to use guardianship under the Mental Health Act or to apply to the Court of Protection for a declaration (see Chapter 12).

Consent to treatment under the Mental Health Act 1983

Section 28 of the Mental Capacity Act states:

> *(1) Nothing in this Act authorises anyone –*
>
> > *(a) to give a patient medical treatment for mental disorder, or*
> >
> > *(b) to consent to a patient's being given medical treatment for mental disorder,*
>
> *if, at the time when it is proposed to treat the patient, his treatment is regulated by Part 4 of the Mental Health Act.*
>
> *(2) 'Medical treatment', 'mental disorder' and 'patient' have the same meaning as in that Act.*

Patients not covered by Part 4 of the Act are in the same position as any other patients in any hospital and cannot be treated without their consent except where the Mental Capacity Act will allow it. In addition, not all detained patients are included. Generally, those patients liable to detention under the Mental Health Act 1983 for periods of more than 72 hours are covered (e.g. ss 2 and 3), with the exception of people remanded for reports by the courts under s 35.

Part 4 of the Mental Health Act outlines the circumstances in which treatment for mental disorder may be given without the consent of a detained patient. The main principle adopted by the Act is that there are some patients who are liable to be detained who may need to be given treatment without their consent. Further, this may be seen as reasonable given the fact of their detention. However, certain safeguards were seen as necessary and were introduced by the 1983 Act.

Some more serious forms of treatment are subject to procedures which should be followed to offer these safeguards. These essentially involve a second medical opinion from outside the hospital in those cases where valid consent cannot be obtained from the patient. This absence of consent could either be the result of the patient objecting to the treatment, or of their being unable to give valid consent (e.g. because of mental incapacity). For the most serious treatments (such as psychosurgery), a second opinion *and* the consent of the patient are required. Because of the invasive nature of these treatments, the safeguards are also extended to informal patients.

The Mental Health Act Commission has a general duty to oversee the operation of this part of the Act.

Other links with the Mental Health Act 1983 and the changes due in 2009

The nearest relative under the Mental Health Act 1983 has certain specific powers such as being able to apply for detention, or to exercise discharge powers and they also have rights to information and to be consulted. It is possible that a nearest relative might also have an LPA for an individual or there may a conflict of opinion between a nearest relative and someone with an LPA or who is acting as a deputy. For a fuller description of this and how other Mental Health Act provisions operate in practice readers are referred to two books in the same series as this text, *The Approved Social Worker's Guide to Psychiatry and Medication* and *The Approved Social Worker's Guide to Mental Health Law*.

The changes to the 1983 Act arising from the Mental Health Act 2007 are expected to take effect in April 2009. Staff will need to be alert to certain significant changes which will occur, such as the ability of a person to make an effective advance decision on ECT.

Links with the children's law

In general the Mental Capacity Act does not apply to children under the age of 16. However, the criminal offence of ill-treatment or wilful neglect under s 44 will apply if the child's incapacity meets the Act's definition (particularly in relation to its cause). Further, the Court of Protection could make an order in relation to the property and affairs of a child if it was persuaded that this was necessary because the child would continue to lack capacity beyond the age of 18 (s 18(3)).

The Act broadly applies to 16 and 17 year olds, but with a few exceptions:

- no one may make or be appointed under an LPA if under the age of 18;

- the court cannot make a statutory will for an under 18 year old;

- an under 18 year old cannot make an advance decision;

- the 'Bournewood gap' provisions when in force will only apply to those over the age of 18.

So health and social care professionals will still be faced with a number of possible routes to take in relation to an under 18 year old:

- the Children Act 1989;

- the Mental Health Act 1983;

- the Mental Capacity Act 2005; and indeed

- the common law and the inherent jurisdiction of the High Court.

The need for relief to extend beyond the child's 18th birthday will no doubt encourage application to the Court of Protection under the Mental Capacity Act rather than using the Children Act but transfer between jurisdictions will be straightforward (under the Mental Capacity Act 2005 (Transfer of Proceedings) Order 2007 No. 1899) should this subsequently become appropriate. The considerations to be borne in mind in determining the route will remain largely unaltered, particularly in relation to the choice between the Mental Health Act and the Children Act.

More detailed consideration of this area of potential overlap is outside the scope of this book and practitioners are referred to Chapter 12 of the Code of Practice to the Mental Capacity Act and to a forthcoming text on mental disorder, children and the law by Harbour (2008).

Links with the common law

Some practitioners struggle with the concept of common law. Although many social workers' tasks are rooted firmly in statute there are frequent overlaps with the common law. It is therefore necessary for social workers to have a working grasp of what is meant by common law and how it might relate to their practice. The *Oxford Dictionary of Law* (2006, p.104) gives three basic definitions of common law:

1. *The part of English law based on rules developed by the royal courts during the first three centuries after the Norman Conquest (1066) as a system applicable to the whole country, as opposed to local customs. . .*

2. *Rules of law developed by the courts as opposed to those created by statute.*

3. *A general system of law deriving exclusively from court decisions.*

Montgomery (2002, p.7) has described common law as:

The rules which are extrapolated from the practice of the judges in deciding cases.

Some practitioners have referred to this as 'common sense under a wig'.

The Mental Capacity Act takes, adapts and clothes in statutory form a number of areas of common (judge-made) law, in particular:

- the test for incapacity;

- the means of establishing 'best interests';

- the authority to intervene in relation to a person lacking capacity and the limits to that authority;

- the law relating to advance decisions.

So for many areas of practice what used to be common law is now covered by the statute. Just when the common law will continue to apply in relation to dealing with those lacking capacity is an interesting issue and outside the scope of this book. What is left of the common law will depend to some extent upon how the courts construe the Mental Capacity Act, whether broadly or narrowly. Perhaps the safest advice would be to confine the use of common law powers in relation to a person lacking capacity to emergencies and short-term interventions.

ACTIVITY **15.1**

Multiple choice questions

Read each question carefully and tick the appropriate box(es). Where a statement is correct, tick the box next to it; if it is incorrect, leave it blank. You may need to tick more than one box per question.

Appendix 5 (pages 145–9) gives the answers.

15.1 *'An impairment of, or a disturbance in the functioning of, the mind or brain' is a key phrase to be found in* **BOTH** *the Mental Health Act 2007 and the Mental Capacity Act 2005:*

(a) *True* ☐

(b) *False* ☐

15.2 *In HL v UK the European Court ruled that there had been breaches of:*

(a) *Article 3 – prohibition of torture* ☐

(b) *Article 5.1 – right to liberty and security of person* ☐

(c) *Article 5.4 – right to a speedy review of detention* ☐

(d) *Article 8.1 – right to respect for private and family life* ☐

(e) *Article 12 – right to marry and found a family* ☐

(f) *Article 14 – prohibition of discrimination* ☐

15.3 *The Mental Capacity Act limits the following areas to people of 18 or over:*

(a) *making an advance decision* ☐

(b) *any intervention under s 5 on the basis of mental incapacity* ☐

(c) *making a Lasting Power of Attorney* ☐

(d) *being a named person for consultation as part of the best interests checklist* ☐

(e) *becoming an attorney under a Lasting Power of Attorney* ☐

(f) *use of the new Bournewood safeguards when implemented* ☐

Chapter 16

The 'Bournewood' provisions

Introduction

The Mental Health Act 2007 has been used as a vehicle to amend the Mental Capacity Act in order to make new provisions for those individuals who are seen as 'Bournewood' type patients. This includes those people who are in hospital, and are compliant, but lack capacity in relation to the decision to be in hospital, and are in effect deprived of their liberty. The provisions have also been used to cover mentally disordered people who are in care homes or nursing homes under conditions which would amount to deprivation of liberty. The dilemma for this latter group has been that in many cases it would not be appropriate to detain the person under the Mental Health Act as they would not be suitably placed in a hospital. Guardianship would be an alternative but there are still some doubts as to whether this is sufficient to justify deprivation of liberty. In the recent case of *JE v DE (1), Surrey CC (2)*, 2006 the judge used the phrase 'not free to leave' when he ruled that JE had been deprived of his liberty. Patients subject to guardianship could be described as not free to leave so this case has raised the question of whether indeed guardianship could be considered in such cases as it provides a procedure prescribed by law.

The new parts of the Act had not been put into effect at the time this book was going to press and so they have been included here in a separate chapter. They are expected to operate from April 2009 but readers will need to check that this is the case. There is a tendency for target dates to be put back, as with the commencement of the main parts of the Mental Capacity Act.

Court decisions

Additions to s 4 will allow for a deprivation of liberty where this is giving effect to a relevant court decision. This is covering the situation where, for example, someone falls outside the remit of the Mental Health Act and therefore cannot be detained under that Act. The Court of Protection might then make a declaration that the person lacks capacity in relation to the decision regarding hospital admission and that they should be admitted and that this will involve a deprivation of liberty. Possibly more likely is that the Court of Protection will make personal welfare decisions under s 16.

The need for the court to fill this gap in the Mental Health Act could arise with a person with learning disabilities. They may be vulnerable to abuse or neglect, but are not abnormally aggressive or seriously irresponsible. They could not therefore be seen as 'mentally impaired' as defined by the Mental Health Act, which in turn would mean that they could not be detained beyond 28 days. For the first 28 days they could be detained under s 2 as they have 'arrested or incomplete development of mind' which is a sufficient form of mental disorder for this short-term detention but not for a s 3 detention. Equally they could not be received into guardianship. Even when the definition of mental disorder changes (this is expected in April 2009) this problem will remain, as such patients will still be excluded from long-term compulsion under the Mental Health Act. Before the Mental Capacity Act came into effect such cases had to be referred to the High Court. They will now be referred to the Court of Protection. The amended s 4 will allow people to act on a declaration from the Court of Protection authorising deprivation of liberty in such circumstances.

A new authorisation procedure

The new Schedules to the Mental Capacity Act allow for certain people to be deprived of their liberty without the use of the Mental Health Act and without needing to apply to the Court of Protection.

Where a care home, nursing home or hospital has a person who is deprived of liberty within their care (or they are likely to be deprived of their liberty within the next 28 days) they must apply for an authorisation of deprivation of liberty.

In the case of a care home the application must be made to the local authority where the person is ordinarily resident or, if there is some uncertainty or dispute as to where the person is normally resident, the local authority where the care home is sited. If there is a question about where a person is ordinarily resident it is to be determined by the Secretary of State or the National Assembly for Wales.

In England applications will be made to the relevant Primary Care Trust when the patient is in hospital, or to the local authority when the person is in a care home. In Wales applications for people in hospital will be made to the National Assembly. The PCT, National Assembly or local authority are referred to as the 'supervisory authority', whilst the managers of the establishment where the person is staying are referred to as the 'managing authority'.

The managing authority applies to the supervisory authority (i.e. the PCT or National Assembly or local authority) for authorisation of deprivation of liberty.

The supervisory authority then commissions six assessments: age; mental health; mental capacity; best interests; eligibility; and no refusals. These assessments must involve at least two assessors, as the mental disorder and the best interests assessments must be carried out by different people.

If all the assessments are positive the supervisory body can approve deprivation of liberty up to a maximum of one year.

The six requirements

1. Age. The person must be 18 or older. (Note that s 25 of the Children Act 1989 would apply to those under 18.)

2. Mental health. The person needs to have a mental disorder as defined by the Mental Health Act 1983. It is likely to be doctors approved under s 12 of that Act who carry this out this test. Note that the 'abnormally aggressive or seriously irresponsible conduct' test does *not* apply in this situation. This would, therefore, allow the deprivation of liberty of some people with learning disabilities who would not be detainable long term under the Mental Health Act. The fact that people with no mental disorder at all will not be able to be deprived of their liberty under this provision could lead to confusion. It remains to be seen which diagnoses will be seen as leading to mental incapacity but which are not mental disorders. The draft revisions to the Code of Practice were silent on this issue. In any event, the result will be that for any such people an application would have to be made to the Court of Protection.

3. Mental capacity. The person must lack capacity to make a decision to be accommodated in the hospital, nursing home or care home for the relevant care or treatment.

4. Best interests. It is likely to be Approved Social Workers (possibly transformed into Approved Mental Health Practitioners by the time this is implemented) or care co-ordinators who carry out this test. It includes the following conditions:

(i) The person is, or is to be, a detained resident

(ii) It is in their best interests to be a detained resident

(iii) In order to prevent harm to that person it is necessary for him to be a detained resident.

Note that this would not include harm to others.

It also needs to be a proportionate response to the likelihood of the relevant person suffering harm, and the seriousness of that harm, for him to be a detained resident.

5. Eligibility. The person must not be subject to Mental Health Act compulsion. This will require a check that there is no guardianship order, Community Treatment Order, or s 17 leave based on a liability to be detained under the Mental Health Act. The new Schedule 1A to the Act also states that a person will be ineligible for an authorisation under these new procedures if they are an informal mental health patient who objects to either:

(a) being a mental health patient, or

(b) being given some or all of the mental health treatment.

One might have thought this would have counted as a refusal but it is separated from that concept and is included under eligibility.

6. No refusals. There must be no valid refusal to the decision concerning the person's residence from someone in a position of authority such as a donee of a Lasting Power of Attorney or a deputy appointed by the Court of Protection.

For someone being treated in a hospital there must be no objection from the person themselves. In these circumstances there should be an assessment carried out under the Mental Health Act.

Authorisation of deprivation of liberty

If all six conditions are met the following points apply:

- authorisation must be in writing and include the purpose of the deprivation of liberty, the time period, any conditions recommended by the best interests assessor, and the reasons that each of the assessment criteria are met;

- the supervisory body appoints a representative for the person (usually on the recommendation of the best interests assessor);

- any appeals are to the Court of Protection.

Where a standard authorisation has been given the court may determine any question relating to any of the following matters:

(a) whether the relevant person meets one or more of the qualifying requirements;

(b) the period during which the standard authorisation is given;

(c) the purpose for which the standard authorisation is given;

(d) the conditions to which the standard authorisation is given.

The court also has powers in relation to urgent authorisations and determination of liability.

The Department of Health has predicted that there may be as many as 20–30,000 assessments in the first year of operating this new procedure, and that numbers should then fall. This is a rather conservative estimate when compared with the 48,000 people that the Department of Health thought would be affected by the *HL* case when it was going through the domestic courts. It is very difficult to anticipate precisely what effect the new procedures will have. There are clearly significant workforce planning issues with these new proposals and this may affect the timing of the implementation of the new procedures. It could also be argued that these rather bureaucratic procedures sit rather uncomfortably in an Act designed to be enabling and supportive of people who lack capacity.

Deprivation of liberty necessary for life-sustaining treatment etc.

A new section 4B states:

> *(1) If the following conditions are met, D is authorised to deprive P of his liberty while a decision as respects any relevant issue is sought from the court.*

> *(2) The first condition is that there is a question about whether D is authorised to deprive P of his liberty under section 4A.*

(3) The second condition is that the deprivation of liberty –

   (a) is wholly or partly for the purpose of –

      (i) giving P life-sustaining treatment, or

      (ii) doing any vital act, or

   (b) consists wholly or partly of –

      (i) giving P life-sustaining treatment, or

      (ii) doing any vital act.

(4) The third condition is that the deprivation of liberty is necessary in order to –

   (a) give the life-sustaining treatment, or

   (b) do the vital act.

(5) A vital act is any act which the person doing it reasonably believes to be necessary to prevent a serious deterioration in P's condition.

It is hoped that this new provision will reassure medical staff faced with a patient who is incapacitated in relation to a life-sustaining treatment or one that would prevent a serious deterioration in his condition. If they are seeking a decision from the court they will be able to treat whilst waiting for the decision even if this is going to involve deprivation of liberty. It needs to be emphasised that a court application must be in train for this provision to be used. Doctors cannot just treat in an emergency and then decide not to take the issue to court. What amounts to a deprivation of liberty in some cases where the central issue concerns the imposition of medical treatment may be hard to determine in practice.

Urgent authorisation of deprivation of liberty

In an emergency there can be an urgent authorisation of up to seven days. The reasons for this authorisation need to be recorded.

ACTIVITY *16.1*

Multiple choice questions

Read each question carefully and tick the appropriate box(es). Where a statement is correct, tick the box next to it; if it is incorrect, leave it blank. You may need to tick more than one box per question.

Appendix 5 (pages 145–9) gives the answers.

16.1 The Government now plans to introduce measures to close the 'Bournewood gap'. For relevant cases supervisory bodies will commission which of the following assessments:

(a) Best interests ☐

(b) Objections (e.g. from LPA) ☐

(c) Age ☐

(d) Financial ☐

(e) Eligibility ☐

(f) Whether receiving MH Act s 117 after-care ☐

(g) Mental capacity ☐

(h) Abnormally aggressive or seriously irresponsible conduct ☐

(i) Mental health ☐

16.2 Under the new 'Bournewood' measures one professional could carry out all of the required assessments:

(a) True ☐

(b) False ☐

16.3 Under the new 'Bournewood' measures a representative will be appointed for the individual after deprivation of liberty has been authorised:

(a) True ☐

(b) False ☐

Appendices

Appendix 1 The Mental Capacity Act 2005

Contents

Part 1   Persons who lack capacity

Powers of the court in relation to lasting powers of attorney

Advance decisions to refuse treatment

Excluded decisions

Research

Independent mental capacity advocate service

Miscellaneous and supplementary

Part 2   The Court of Protection and the Public Guardian

The Court of Protection

Supplementary powers

Part 3   Miscellaneous and general

Mental Capacity Act 2005

Part 1   Persons who lack capacity

The principles

1   The principles

(1) The following principles apply for the purposes of this Act.

(2) A person must be assumed to have capacity unless it is established that he lacks capacity.

(3) A person is not to be treated as unable to make a decision unless all practicable steps to help him to do so have been taken without success.

(4) A person is not to be treated as unable to make a decision merely because he makes an unwise decision.

(5) An act done, or decision made, under this Act for or on behalf of a person who lacks capacity must be done, or made, in his best interests.

(6) Before the act is done, or the decision is made, regard must be had to whether the purpose for which it is needed can be as effectively achieved in a way that is less restrictive of the person's rights and freedom of action.

Preliminary

2   People who lack capacity

(1) For the purposes of this Act, a person lacks capacity in relation to a matter if at the material time he is unable to make a decision for himself in relation to the matter because of an impairment of, or a disturbance in the functioning of, the mind or brain.

(2) It does not matter whether the impairment or disturbance is permanent or temporary.

(3) A lack of capacity cannot be established merely by reference to –
  (a) a person's age or appearance, or
  (b) a condition of his, or an aspect of his behaviour, which might lead others to make unjustified assumptions about his capacity.

(4) In proceedings under this Act or any other enactment, any question whether a person lacks capacity within the meaning of this Act must be decided on the balance of probabilities.

(5) No power which a person ('D') may exercise under this Act –
  (a) in relation to a person who lacks capacity, or
  (b) where D reasonably thinks that a person lacks capacity,
is exercisable in relation to a person under 16.

(6) Subsection (5) is subject to section 18(3).

3 Inability to make decisions

(1) For the purposes of section 2, a person is unable to make a decision for himself if he is unable –

    (a) to understand the information relevant to the decision,

    (b) to retain that information,

    (c) to use or weigh that information as part of the process of making the decision, or

    (d) to communicate his decision (whether by talking, using sign language or any other means).

(2) A person is not to be regarded as unable to understand the information relevant to a decision if he is able to understand an explanation of it given to him in a way that is appropriate to his circumstances (using simple language, visual aids or any other means).

(3) The fact that a person is able to retain the information relevant to a decision for a short period only does not prevent him from being regarded as able to make the decision.

(4) The information relevant to a decision includes information about the reasonably foreseeable consequences of –

    (a) deciding one way or another, or

    (b) failing to make the decision.

4 Best interests

(1) In determining for the purposes of this Act what is in a person's best interests, the person making the determination must not make it merely on the basis of –

    (a) the person's age or appearance, or

    (b) a condition of his, or an aspect of his behaviour, which might lead others to make unjustified assumptions about what might be in his best interests.

(2) The person making the determination must consider all the relevant circumstances and, in particular, take the following steps.

(3) He must consider –

    (a) whether it is likely that the person will at some time have capacity in relation to the matter in question, and

    (b) if it appears likely that he will, when that is likely to be.

(4) He must, so far as reasonably practicable, permit and encourage the person to participate, or to improve his ability to participate, as fully as possible in any act done for him and any decision affecting him.

(5) Where the determination relates to life-sustaining treatment he must not, in considering whether the treatment is in the best interests of the person concerned, be motivated by a desire to bring about his death.

(6) He must consider, so far as is reasonably ascertainable –

    (a) the person's past and present wishes and feelings (and, in particular, any relevant written statement made by him when he had capacity),

    (b) the beliefs and values that would be likely to influence his decision if he had capacity, and

    (c) the other factors that he would be likely to consider if he were able to do so.

(7) He must take into account, if it is practicable and appropriate to consult them, the views of –

(a) anyone named by the person as someone to be consulted on the matter in question or on matters of that kind,

(b) anyone engaged in caring for the person or interested in his welfare,

(c) any donee of a lasting power of attorney granted by the person, and

(d) any deputy appointed for the person by the court,

as to what would be in the person's best interests and, in particular, as to the matters mentioned in subsection (6).

(8) The duties imposed by subsections (1) to (7) also apply in relation to the exercise of any powers which –

(a) are exercisable under a lasting power of attorney, or

(b) are exercisable by a person under this Act where he reasonably believes that another person lacks capacity.

(9) In the case of an act done, or a decision made, by a person other than the court, there is sufficient compliance with this section if (having complied with the requirements of subsections (1) to (7)) he reasonably believes that what he does or decides is in the best interests of the person concerned.

(10) 'Life-sustaining treatment' means treatment which in the view of a person providing health care for the person concerned is necessary to sustain life.

(11) 'Relevant circumstances' are those –

(a) of which the person making the determination is aware, and

(b) which it would be reasonable to regard as relevant.

5   Acts in connection with care or treatment

(1) If a person ('D') does an act in connection with the care or treatment of another person ('P'), the act is one to which this section applies if –

(a) before doing the act, D takes reasonable steps to establish whether P lacks capacity in relation to the matter in question, and

(b) when doing the act, D reasonably believes –

(i) that P lacks capacity in relation to the matter, and

(ii) that it will be in P's best interests for the act to be done.

(2) D does not incur any liability in relation to the act that he would not have incurred if P –

(a) had had capacity to consent in relation to the matter, and

(b) had consented to D's doing the act.

(3) Nothing in this section excludes a person's civil liability for loss or damage, or his criminal liability, resulting from his negligence in doing the act.

(4) Nothing in this section affects the operation of sections 24 to 26 (advance decisions to refuse treatment).

6   Section 5 acts: limitations

(1) If D does an act that is intended to restrain P, it is not an act to which section 5 applies unless two further conditions are satisfied.

(2) The first condition is that D reasonably believes that it is necessary to do the act in order to prevent harm to P.

(3) The second is that the act is a proportionate response to –

(a) the likelihood of P's suffering harm, and

(b) the seriousness of that harm.

(4) For the purposes of this section D restrains P if he –

  (a) uses, or threatens to use, force to secure the doing of an act which P resists, or

  (b) restricts P's liberty of movement, whether or not P resists.

(5) But D does more than merely restrain P if he deprives P of his liberty within the meaning of Article 5(1) of the Human Rights Convention (whether or not D is a public authority).

(6) Section 5 does not authorise a person to do an act which conflicts with a decision made, within the scope of his authority and in accordance with this Part, by –

  (a) a donee of a lasting power of attorney granted by P, or

  (b) a deputy appointed for P by the court.

(7) But nothing in subsection (6) stops a person –

  (a) providing life-sustaining treatment, or

  (b) doing any act which he reasonably believes to be necessary to prevent a serious deterioration in P's condition,

while a decision as respects any relevant issue is sought from the court.

7 Payment for necessary goods and services

(1) If necessary goods or services are supplied to a person who lacks capacity to contract for the supply, he must pay a reasonable price for them.

(2) 'Necessary' means suitable to a person's condition in life and to his actual requirements at the time when the goods or services are supplied.

8 Expenditure

(1) If an act to which section 5 applies involves expenditure, it is lawful for D –

  (a) to pledge P's credit for the purpose of the expenditure, and

  (b) to apply money in P's possession for meeting the expenditure.

(2) If the expenditure is borne for P by D, it is lawful for D –

  (a) to reimburse himself out of money in P's possession, or

  (b) to be otherwise indemnified by P.

(3) Subsections (1) and (2) do not affect any power under which (apart from those subsections) a person –

  (a) has lawful control of P's money or other property, and

  (b) has power to spend money for P's benefit.

Lasting powers of attorney

9 Lasting powers of attorney

(1) A lasting power of attorney is a power of attorney under which the donor ('P') confers on the donee (or donees) authority to make decisions about all or any of the following –

  (a) P's personal welfare or specified matters concerning P's personal welfare, and

  (b) P's property and affairs or specified matters concerning P's property and affairs,

and which includes authority to make such decisions in circumstances where P no longer has capacity.

(2) A lasting power of attorney is not created unless –

  (a) section 10 is complied with,

(b) an instrument conferring authority of the kind mentioned in subsection (1) is made and registered in accordance with Schedule 1, and

(c) at the time when P executes the instrument, P has reached 18 and has capacity to execute it.

(3) An instrument which –

(a) purports to create a lasting power of attorney, but

(b) does not comply with this section, section 10 or Schedule 1,

confers no authority.

(4) The authority conferred by a lasting power of attorney is subject to –

(a) the provisions of this Act and, in particular, sections 1 (the principles) and 4 (best interests), and

(b) any conditions or restrictions specified in the instrument.

10 Appointment of donees

(1) A donee of a lasting power of attorney must be –

(a) an individual who has reached 18, or

(b) if the power relates only to P's property and affairs, either such an individual or a trust corporation.

(2) An individual who is bankrupt may not be appointed as donee of a lasting power of attorney in relation to P's property and affairs.

(3) Subsections (4) to (7) apply in relation to an instrument under which two or more persons are to act as donees of a lasting power of attorney.

(4) The instrument may appoint them to act –

(a) jointly,

(b) jointly and severally, or

(c) jointly in respect of some matters and jointly and severally in respect of others.

(5) To the extent to which it does not specify whether they are to act jointly or jointly and severally, the instrument is to be assumed to appoint them to act jointly.

(6) If they are to act jointly, a failure, as respects one of them, to comply with the requirements of subsection (1) or (2) or Part 1 or 2 of Schedule 1 prevents a lasting power of attorney from being created.

(7) If they are to act jointly and severally, a failure, as respects one of them, to comply with the requirements of subsection (1) or (2) or Part 1 or 2 of Schedule 1 –

(a) prevents the appointment taking effect in his case, but

(b) does not prevent a lasting power of attorney from being created in the case of the other or others.

(8) An instrument used to create a lasting power of attorney –

(a) cannot give the donee (or, if more than one, any of them) power to appoint a substitute or successor, but

(b) may itself appoint a person to replace the donee (or, if more than one, any of them) on the occurrence of an event mentioned in section 13(6)(a) to (d) which has the effect of terminating the donee's appointment.

11 Lasting powers of attorney: restrictions

(1) A lasting power of attorney does not authorise the donee (or, if more than one, any of them) to do an act that is intended to restrain P, unless three conditions are satisfied.

(2) The first condition is that P lacks, or the donee reasonably believes that P lacks, capacity in relation to the matter in question.

(3) The second is that the donee reasonably believes that it is necessary to do the act in order to prevent harm to P.

(4) The third is that the act is a proportionate response to –
  (a) the likelihood of P's suffering harm, and
  (b) the seriousness of that harm.

(5) For the purposes of this section, the donee restrains P if he –
  (a) uses, or threatens to use, force to secure the doing of an act which P resists, or
  (b) restricts P's liberty of movement, whether or not P resists,
or if he authorises another person to do any of those things.

(6) But the donee does more than merely restrain P if he deprives P of his liberty within the meaning of Article 5(1) of the Human Rights Convention.

(7) Where a lasting power of attorney authorises the donee (or, if more than one, any of them) to make decisions about P's personal welfare, the authority –
  (a) does not extend to making such decisions in circumstances other than those where P lacks, or the donee reasonably believes that P lacks, capacity,
  (b) is subject to sections 24 to 26 (advance decisions to refuse treatment), and
  (c) extends to giving or refusing consent to the carrying out or continuation of a treatment by a person providing health care for P.

(8) But subsection (7)(c) –
  (a) does not authorise the giving or refusing of consent to the carrying out or continuation of life-sustaining treatment, unless the instrument contains express provision to that effect, and
  (b) is subject to any conditions or restrictions in the instrument.

12 Scope of lasting powers of attorney: gifts

(1) Where a lasting power of attorney confers authority to make decisions about P's property and affairs, it does not authorise a donee (or, if more than one, any of them) to dispose of the donor's property by making gifts except to the extent permitted by subsection (2).

(2) The donee may make gifts –
  (a) on customary occasions to persons (including himself) who are related to or connected with the donor, or
  (b) to any charity to whom the donor made or might have been expected to make gifts,
if the value of each such gift is not unreasonable having regard to all the circumstances and, in particular, the size of the donor's estate.

(3) 'Customary occasion' means –
  (a) the occasion or anniversary of a birth, a marriage or the formation of a civil partnership, or
  (b) any other occasion on which presents are customarily given within families or among friends or associates.

(4) Subsection (2) is subject to any conditions or restrictions in the instrument.

13   Revocation of lasting powers of attorney etc.

(1) This section applies if –

(a) P has executed an instrument with a view to creating a lasting power of attorney, or

(b) a lasting power of attorney is registered as having been conferred by P,

and in this section references to revoking the power include revoking the instrument.

(2) P may, at any time when he has capacity to do so, revoke the power.

(3) P's bankruptcy revokes the power so far as it relates to P's property and affairs.

(4) But where P is bankrupt merely because an interim bankruptcy restrictions order has effect in respect of him, the power is suspended, so far as it relates to P's property and affairs, for so long as the order has effect.

(5) The occurrence in relation to a donee of an event mentioned in subsection (6) –

(a) terminates his appointment, and

(b) except in the cases given in subsection (7), revokes the power.

(6) The events are –

(a) the disclaimer of the appointment by the donee in accordance with such requirements as may be prescribed for the purposes of this section in regulations made by the Lord Chancellor,

(b) subject to subsections (8) and (9), the death or bankruptcy of the donee or, if the donee is a trust corporation, its winding-up or dissolution,

(c) subject to subsection (11), the dissolution or annulment of a marriage or civil partnership between the donor and the donee,

(d) the lack of capacity of the donee.

(7) The cases are –

(a) the donee is replaced under the terms of the instrument,

(b) he is one of two or more persons appointed to act as donees jointly and severally in respect of any matter and, after the event, there is at least one remaining donee.

(8) The bankruptcy of a donee does not terminate his appointment, or revoke the power, in so far as his authority relates to P's personal welfare.

(9) Where the donee is bankrupt merely because an interim bankruptcy restrictions order has effect in respect of him, his appointment and the power are suspended, so far as they relate to P's property and affairs, for so long as the order has effect.

(10) Where the donee is one of two or more appointed to act jointly and severally under the power in respect of any matter, the reference in subsection (9) to the suspension of the power is to its suspension in so far as it relates to that donee.

(11) The dissolution or annulment of a marriage or civil partnership does not terminate the appointment of a donee, or revoke the power, if the instrument provided that it was not to do so.

14   Protection of donee and others if no power created or power revoked

(1) Subsections (2) and (3) apply if –

(a) an instrument has been registered under Schedule 1 as a lasting power of attorney, but

(b) a lasting power of attorney was not created,

whether or not the registration has been cancelled at the time of the act or transaction in question.

(2) A donee who acts in purported exercise of the power does not incur any liability (to P or any other person) because of the non-existence of the power unless at the time of acting he –

    (a) knows that a lasting power of attorney was not created, or

    (b) is aware of circumstances which, if a lasting power of attorney had been created, would have terminated his authority to act as a donee.

(3) Any transaction between the donee and another person is, in favour of that person, as valid as if the power had been in existence, unless at the time of the transaction that person has knowledge of a matter referred to in subsection (2).

(4) If the interest of a purchaser depends on whether a transaction between the donee and the other person was valid by virtue of subsection (3), it is conclusively presumed in favour of the purchaser that the transaction was valid if –

    (a) the transaction was completed within 12 months of the date on which the instrument was registered, or

    (b) the other person makes a statutory declaration, before or within 3 months after the completion of the purchase, that he had no reason at the time of the transaction to doubt that the donee had authority to dispose of the property which was the subject of the transaction.

(5) In its application to a lasting power of attorney which relates to matters in addition to P's property and affairs, section 5 of the Powers of Attorney Act 1971 (c. 27) (protection where power is revoked) has effect as if references to revocation included the cessation of the power in relation to P's property and affairs.

(6) Where two or more donees are appointed under a lasting power of attorney, this section applies as if references to the donee were to all or any of them.

General powers of the court and appointment of deputies

15   Power to make declarations

(1) The court may make declarations as to –

    (a) whether a person has or lacks capacity to make a decision specified in the declaration;

    (b) whether a person has or lacks capacity to make decisions on such matters as are described in the declaration;

    (c) the lawfulness or otherwise of any act done, or yet to be done, in relation to that person.

(2) 'Act' includes an omission and a course of conduct.

16   Powers to make decisions and appoint deputies: general

(1) This section applies if a person ('P') lacks capacity in relation to a matter or matters concerning –

    (a) P's personal welfare, or

    (b) P's property and affairs.

(2) The court may –

    (a) by making an order, make the decision or decisions on P's behalf in relation to the matter or matters, or

    (b) appoint a person (a 'deputy') to make decisions on P's behalf in relation to the matter or matters.

(3) The powers of the court under this section are subject to the provisions of this Act and, in particular, to sections 1 (the principles) and 4 (best interests).

(4) When deciding whether it is in P's best interests to appoint a deputy, the court must have regard (in addition to the matters mentioned in section 4) to the principles that –

    (a) a decision by the court is to be preferred to the appointment of a deputy to make a decision, and

    (b) the powers conferred on a deputy should be as limited in scope and duration as is reasonably practicable in the circumstances.

(5) The court may make such further orders or give such directions, and confer on a deputy such powers or impose on him such duties, as it thinks necessary or expedient for giving effect to, or otherwise in connection with, an order or appointment made by it under subsection (2).

(6) Without prejudice to section 4, the court may make the order, give the directions or make the appointment on such terms as it considers are in P's best interests, even though no application is before the court for an order, directions or an appointment on those terms.

(7) An order of the court may be varied or discharged by a subsequent order.

(8) The court may, in particular, revoke the appointment of a deputy or vary the powers conferred on him if it is satisfied that the deputy –

    (a) has behaved, or is behaving, in a way that contravenes the authority conferred on him by the court or is not in P's best interests, or

    (b) proposes to behave in a way that would contravene that authority or would not be in P's best interests.

17   Section 16 powers: personal welfare

(1) The powers under section 16 as respects P's personal welfare extend in particular to –

    (a) deciding where P is to live;

    (b) deciding what contact, if any, P is to have with any specified persons;

    (c) making an order prohibiting a named person from having contact with P;

    (d) giving or refusing consent to the carrying out or continuation of a treatment by a person providing health care for P;

    (e) giving a direction that a person responsible for P's health care allow a different person to take over that responsibility.

(2) Subsection (1) is subject to section 20 (restrictions on deputies).

18   Section 16 powers: property and affairs

(1) The powers under section 16 as respects P's property and affairs extend in particular to –

    (a) the control and management of P's property;

    (b) the sale, exchange, charging, gift or other disposition of P's property;

    (c) the acquisition of property in P's name or on P's behalf;

    (d) the carrying on, on P's behalf, of any profession, trade or business;

    (e) the taking of a decision which will have the effect of dissolving a partnership of which P is a member;

    (f) the carrying out of any contract entered into by P;

    (g) the discharge of P's debts and of any of P's obligations, whether legally enforce-able or not;

    (h) the settlement of any of P's property, whether for P's benefit or for the benefit of others;

    (i) the execution for P of a will;

    (j) the exercise of any power (including a power to consent) vested in P whether beneficially or as trustee or otherwise;

    (k) the conduct of legal proceedings in P's name or on P's behalf.

(2) No will may be made under subsection (1)(i) at a time when P has not reached 18.

(3) The powers under section 16 as respects any other matter relating to P's property and affairs may be exercised even though P has not reached 16, if the court considers it likely that P will still lack capacity to make decisions in respect of that matter when he reaches 18.

(4) Schedule 2 supplements the provisions of this section.

(5) Section 16(7) (variation and discharge of court orders) is subject to paragraph 6 of Schedule 2.

(6) Subsection (1) is subject to section 20 (restrictions on deputies).

19 Appointment of deputies

(1) A deputy appointed by the court must be –

    (a) an individual who has reached 18, or

    (b) as respects powers in relation to property and affairs, an individual who has reached 18 or a trust corporation.

(2) The court may appoint an individual by appointing the holder for the time being of a specified office or position.

(3) A person may not be appointed as a deputy without his consent.

(4) The court may appoint two or more deputies to act –

    (a) jointly,

    (b) jointly and severally, or

    (c) jointly in respect of some matters and jointly and severally in respect of others.

(5) When appointing a deputy or deputies, the court may at the same time appoint one or more other persons to succeed the existing deputy or those deputies –

    (a) in such circumstances, or on the happening of such events, as may be specified by the court;

    (b) for such period as may be so specified.

(6) A deputy is to be treated as P's agent in relation to anything done or decided by him within the scope of his appointment and in accordance with this Part.

(7) The deputy is entitled –

    (a) to be reimbursed out of P's property for his reasonable expenses in discharging his functions, and

    (b) if the court so directs when appointing him, to remuneration out of P's property for discharging them.

(8) The court may confer on a deputy powers to –

    (a) take possession or control of all or any specified part of P's property;

    (b) exercise all or any specified powers in respect of it, including such powers of investment as the court may determine.

(9) The court may require a deputy –
    (a) to give to the Public Guardian such security as the court thinks fit for the due discharge of his functions, and
    (b) to submit to the Public Guardian such reports at such times or at such intervals as the court may direct.

20   Restrictions on deputies

(1) A deputy does not have power to make a decision on behalf of P in relation to a matter if he knows or has reasonable grounds for believing that P has capacity in relation to the matter.

(2) Nothing in section 16(5) or 17 permits a deputy to be given power –
    (a) to prohibit a named person from having contact with P;
    (b) to direct a person responsible for P's health care to allow a different person to take over that responsibility.

(3) A deputy may not be given powers with respect to –
    (a) the settlement of any of P's property, whether for P's benefit or for the benefit of others,
    (b) the execution for P of a will, or
    (c) the exercise of any power (including a power to consent) vested in P whether beneficially or as trustee or otherwise.

(4) A deputy may not be given power to make a decision on behalf of P which is inconsistent with a decision made, within the scope of his authority and in accordance with this Act, by the donee of a lasting power of attorney granted by P (or, if there is more than one donee, by any of them).

(5) A deputy may not refuse consent to the carrying out or continuation of life-sustaining treatment in relation to P.

(6) The authority conferred on a deputy is subject to the provisions of this Act and, in particular, sections 1 (the principles) and 4 (best interests).

(7) A deputy may not do an act that is intended to restrain P unless four conditions are satisfied.

(8) The first condition is that, in doing the act, the deputy is acting within the scope of an authority expressly conferred on him by the court.

(9) The second is that P lacks, or the deputy reasonably believes that P lacks, capacity in relation to the matter in question.

(10) The third is that the deputy reasonably believes that it is necessary to do the act in order to prevent harm to P.

(11) The fourth is that the act is a proportionate response to –
    (a) the likelihood of P's suffering harm, or
    (b) the seriousness of that harm.

(12) For the purposes of this section, a deputy restrains P if he –
    (a) uses, or threatens to use, force to secure the doing of an act which P resists, or
    (b) restricts P's liberty of movement, whether or not P resists,
or if he authorises another person to do any of those things.

(13) But a deputy does more than merely restrain P if he deprives P of his liberty within the meaning of Article 5(1) of the Human Rights Convention (whether or not the deputy is a public authority).

21 Transfer of proceedings relating to people under 18

The Lord Chancellor may by order make provision as to the transfer of proceedings relating to a person under 18, in such circumstances as are specified in the order –

(a) from the Court of Protection to a court having jurisdiction under the Children Act 1989 (c. 41), or

(b) from a court having jurisdiction under that Act to the Court of Protection.

Powers of the court in relation to lasting powers of attorney

22 Powers of court in relation to validity of lasting powers of attorney

(1) This section and section 23 apply if –

(a) a person ('P') has executed or purported to execute an instrument with a view to creating a lasting power of attorney, or

(b) an instrument has been registered as a lasting power of attorney conferred by P.

(2) The court may determine any question relating to –

(a) whether one or more of the requirements for the creation of a lasting power of attorney have been met;

(b) whether the power has been revoked or has otherwise come to an end.

(3) Subsection (4) applies if the court is satisfied –

(a) that fraud or undue pressure was used to induce P –

(i) to execute an instrument for the purpose of creating a lasting power of attorney, or

(ii) to create a lasting power of attorney, or

(b) that the donee (or, if more than one, any of them) of a lasting power of attorney –

(i) has behaved, or is behaving, in a way that contravenes his authority or is not in P's best interests, or

(ii) proposes to behave in a way that would contravene his authority or would not be in P's best interests.

(4) The court may –

(a) direct that an instrument purporting to create the lasting power of attorney is not to be registered, or

(b) if P lacks capacity to do so, revoke the instrument or the lasting power of attorney.

(5) If there is more than one donee, the court may under subsection (4)(b) revoke the instrument or the lasting power of attorney so far as it relates to any of them.

(6) 'Donee' includes an intended donee.

23 Powers of court in relation to operation of lasting powers of attorney

(1) The court may determine any question as to the meaning or effect of a lasting power of attorney or an instrument purporting to create one.

(2) The court may –

(a) give directions with respect to decisions –

(i) which the donee of a lasting power of attorney has authority to make, and

(ii) which P lacks capacity to make;

(b) give any consent or authorisation to act which the donee would have to obtain from P if P had capacity to give it.

(3) The court may, if P lacks capacity to do so –

    (a) give directions to the donee with respect to the rendering by him of reports or accounts and the production of records kept by him for that purpose;

    (b) require the donee to supply information or produce documents or things in his possession as donee;

    (c) give directions with respect to the remuneration or expenses of the donee;

    (d) relieve the donee wholly or partly from any liability which he has or may have incurred on account of a breach of his duties as donee.

(4) The court may authorise the making of gifts which are not within section 12(2) (permitted gifts).

(5) Where two or more donees are appointed under a lasting power of attorney, this section applies as if references to the donee were to all or any of them.

Advance decisions to refuse treatment

24 Advance decisions to refuse treatment: general

(1) 'Advance decision' means a decision made by a person ('P'), after he has reached 18 and when he has capacity to do so, that if –

    (a) at a later time and in such circumstances as he may specify, a specified treatment is proposed to be carried out or continued by a person providing health care for him, and

    (b) at that time he lacks capacity to consent to the carrying out or continuation of the treatment,

the specified treatment is not to be carried out or continued.

(2) For the purposes of subsection (1)(a), a decision may be regarded as specifying a treatment or circumstances even though expressed in layman's terms.

(3) P may withdraw or alter an advance decision at any time when he has capacity to do so.

(4) A withdrawal (including a partial withdrawal) need not be in writing.

(5) An alteration of an advance decision need not be in writing (unless section 25(5) applies in relation to the decision resulting from the alteration).

25 Validity and applicability of advance decisions

(1) An advance decision does not affect the liability which a person may incur for carrying out or continuing a treatment in relation to P unless the decision is at the material time –

    (a) valid, and

    (b) applicable to the treatment.

(2) An advance decision is not valid if P –

    (a) has withdrawn the decision at a time when he had capacity to do so,

    (b) has, under a lasting power of attorney created after the advance decision was made, conferred authority on the donee (or, if more than one, any of them) to give or refuse consent to the treatment to which the advance decision relates, or

    (c) has done anything else clearly inconsistent with the advance decision remaining his fixed decision.

(3) An advance decision is not applicable to the treatment in question if at the material time P has capacity to give or refuse consent to it.

(4) An advance decision is not applicable to the treatment in question if –
    (a) that treatment is not the treatment specified in the advance decision,
    (b) any circumstances specified in the advance decision are absent, or
    (c) there are reasonable grounds for believing that circumstances exist which P did not anticipate at the time of the advance decision and which would have affected his decision had he anticipated them.
(5) An advance decision is not applicable to life-sustaining treatment unless –
    (a) the decision is verified by a statement by P to the effect that it is to apply to that treatment even if life is at risk, and
    (b) the decision and statement comply with subsection (6).
(6) A decision or statement complies with this subsection only if –
    (a) it is in writing,
    (b) it is signed by P or by another person in P's presence and by P's direction,
    (c) the signature is made or acknowledged by P in the presence of a witness, and
    (d) the witness signs it, or acknowledges his signature, in P's presence.
(7) The existence of any lasting power of attorney other than one of a description mentioned in subsection (2)(b) does not prevent the advance decision from being regarded as valid and applicable.

26 Effect of advance decisions

(1) If P has made an advance decision which is –
    (a) valid, and
    (b) applicable to a treatment,
the decision has effect as if he had made it, and had had capacity to make it, at the time when the question arises whether the treatment should be carried out or continued.
(2) A person does not incur liability for carrying out or continuing the treatment unless, at the time, he is satisfied that an advance decision exists which is valid and applicable to the treatment.
(3) A person does not incur liability for the consequences of withholding or withdrawing a treatment from P if, at the time, he reasonably believes that an advance decision exists which is valid and applicable to the treatment.
(4) The court may make a declaration as to whether an advance decision –
    (a) exists;
    (b) is valid;
    (c) is applicable to a treatment.
(5) Nothing in an apparent advance decision stops a person –
    (a) providing life-sustaining treatment, or
    (b) doing any act he reasonably believes to be necessary to prevent a serious deterioration in P's condition,
while a decision as respects any relevant issue is sought from the court.

Excluded decisions

27 Family relationships etc.

(1) Nothing in this Act permits a decision on any of the following matters to be made on behalf of a person –
    (a) consenting to marriage or a civil partnership,

    (b) consenting to have sexual relations,

    (c) consenting to a decree of divorce being granted on the basis of two years' separation,

    (d) consenting to a dissolution order being made in relation to a civil partnership on the basis of two years' separation,

    (e) consenting to a child's being placed for adoption by an adoption agency,

    (f) consenting to the making of an adoption order,

    (g) discharging parental responsibilities in matters not relating to a child's property,

    (h) giving a consent under the Human Fertilisation and Embryology Act 1990 (c. 37).

  (2) 'Adoption order' means –

    (a) an adoption order within the meaning of the Adoption and Children Act 2002 (c. 38) (including a future adoption order), and

    (b) an order under section 84 of that Act (parental responsibility prior to adoption abroad).

28   Mental Health Act matters

  (1) Nothing in this Act authorises anyone –

    (a) to give a patient medical treatment for mental disorder, or

    (b) to consent to a patient's being given medical treatment for mental disorder,

if, at the time when it is proposed to treat the patient, his treatment is regulated by Part 4 of the Mental Health Act.

  (2) 'Medical treatment', 'mental disorder' and 'patient' have the same meaning as in that Act.

29   Voting rights

  (1) Nothing in this Act permits a decision on voting at an election for any public office, or at a referendum, to be made on behalf of a person.

  (2) 'Referendum' has the same meaning as in section 101 of the Political Parties, Elections and Referendums Act 2000 (c. 41).

Research

30   Research

  (1) Intrusive research carried out on, or in relation to, a person who lacks capacity to consent to it is unlawful unless it is carried out –

    (a) as part of a research project which is for the time being approved by the appropriate body for the purposes of this Act in accordance with section 31, and

    (b) in accordance with sections 32 and 33.

  (2) Research is intrusive if it is of a kind that would be unlawful if it was carried out –

    (a) on or in relation to a person who had capacity to consent to it, but

    (b) without his consent.

  (3) A clinical trial which is subject to the provisions of clinical trials regulations is not to be treated as research for the purposes of this section.

  (4) 'Appropriate body', in relation to a research project, means the person, committee or other body specified in regulations made by the appropriate authority as the appropriate body in relation to a project of the kind in question.

(5) 'Clinical trials regulations' means –
    (a) the Medicines for Human Use (Clinical Trials) Regulations 2004 (S.I. 2004/1031) and any other regulations replacing those regulations or amending them, and
    (b) any other regulations relating to clinical trials and designated by the Secretary of State as clinical trials regulations for the purposes of this section.
(6) In this section, section 32 and section 34, 'appropriate authority' means –
    (a) in relation to the carrying out of research in England, the Secretary of State, and
    (b) in relation to the carrying out of research in Wales, the National Assembly for Wales.

31   Requirements for approval

(1) The appropriate body may not approve a research project for the purposes of this Act unless satisfied that the following requirements will be met in relation to research carried out as part of the project on, or in relation to, a person who lacks capacity to consent to taking part in the project ('P').
(2) The research must be connected with –
    (a) an impairing condition affecting P, or
    (b) its treatment.
(3) 'Impairing condition' means a condition which is (or may be) attributable to, or which causes or contributes to (or may cause or contribute to), the impairment of, or disturbance in the functioning of, the mind or brain.
(4) There must be reasonable grounds for believing that research of comparable effectiveness cannot be carried out if the project has to be confined to, or relate only to, persons who have capacity to consent to taking part in it.
(5) The research must –
    (a) have the potential to benefit P without imposing on P a burden that is disproportionate to the potential benefit to P, or
    (b) be intended to provide knowledge of the causes or treatment of, or of the care of persons affected by, the same or a similar condition.
(6) If the research falls within paragraph (b) of subsection (5) but not within paragraph (a), there must be reasonable grounds for believing –
    (a) that the risk to P from taking part in the project is likely to be negligible, and
    (b) that anything done to, or in relation to, P will not –
        (i) interfere with P's freedom of action or privacy in a significant way, or
        (ii) be unduly invasive or restrictive.
(7) There must be reasonable arrangements in place for ensuring that the requirements of sections 32 and 33 will be met.

32   Consulting carers etc.

(1) This section applies if a person ('R') –
    (a) is conducting an approved research project, and
    (b) wishes to carry out research, as part of the project, on or in relation to a person ('P') who lacks capacity to consent to taking part in the project.
(2) R must take reasonable steps to identify a person who –
    (a) otherwise than in a professional capacity or for remuneration, is engaged in caring for P or is interested in P's welfare, and
    (b) is prepared to be consulted by R under this section.

(3) If R is unable to identify such a person he must, in accordance with guidance issued by the appropriate authority, nominate a person who –
    (a) is prepared to be consulted by R under this section, but
    (b) has no connection with the project.

(4) R must provide the person identified under subsection (2), or nominated under subsection (3), with information about the project and ask him –
    (a) for advice as to whether P should take part in the project, and
    (b) what, in his opinion, P's wishes and feelings about taking part in the project would be likely to be if P had capacity in relation to the matter.

(5) If, at any time, the person consulted advises R that in his opinion P's wishes and feelings would be likely to lead him to decline to take part in the project (or to wish to withdraw from it) if he had capacity in relation to the matter, R must ensure –
    (a) if P is not already taking part in the project, that he does not take part in it;
    (b) if P is taking part in the project, that he is withdrawn from it.

(6) But subsection (5)(b) does not require treatment that P has been receiving as part of the project to be discontinued if R has reasonable grounds for believing that there would be a significant risk to P's health if it were discontinued.

(7) The fact that a person is the donee of a lasting power of attorney given by P, or is P's deputy, does not prevent him from being the person consulted under this section.

(8) Subsection (9) applies if treatment is being, or is about to be, provided for P as a matter of urgency and R considers that, having regard to the nature of the research and of the particular circumstances of the case –
    (a) it is also necessary to take action for the purposes of the research as a matter of urgency, but
    (b) it is not reasonably practicable to consult under the previous provisions of this section.

(9) R may take the action if –
    (a) he has the agreement of a registered medical practitioner who is not involved in the organisation or conduct of the research project, or
    (b) where it is not reasonably practicable in the time available to obtain that agreement, he acts in accordance with a procedure approved by the appropriate body at the time when the research project was approved under section 31.

(10) But R may not continue to act in reliance on subsection (9) if he has reasonable grounds for believing that it is no longer necessary to take the action as a matter of urgency.

33 Additional safeguards

(1) This section applies in relation to a person who is taking part in an approved research project even though he lacks capacity to consent to taking part.

(2) Nothing may be done to, or in relation to, him in the course of the research –
    (a) to which he appears to object (whether by showing signs of resistance or otherwise) except where what is being done is intended to protect him from harm or to reduce or prevent pain or discomfort, or
    (b) which would be contrary to –
        (i) an advance decision of his which has effect, or

(ii) any other form of statement made by him and not subsequently withdrawn, of which R is aware.

(3) The interests of the person must be assumed to outweigh those of science and society.

(4) If he indicates (in any way) that he wishes to be withdrawn from the project he must be withdrawn without delay.

(5) P must be withdrawn from the project, without delay, if at any time the person conducting the research has reasonable grounds for believing that one or more of the requirements set out in section 31(2) to (7) is no longer met in relation to research being carried out on, or in relation to, P.

(6) But neither subsection (4) nor subsection (5) requires treatment that P has been receiving as part of the project to be discontinued if R has reasonable grounds for believing that there would be a significant risk to P's health if it were discontinued.

34 Loss of capacity during research project

(1) This section applies where a person ('P') –

   (a) has consented to take part in a research project begun before the commencement of section 30, but

   (b) before the conclusion of the project, loses capacity to consent to continue to take part in it.

(2) The appropriate authority may by regulations provide that, despite P's loss of capacity, research of a prescribed kind may be carried out on, or in relation to, P if –

   (a) the project satisfies prescribed requirements,

   (b) any information or material relating to P which is used in the research is of a prescribed description and was obtained before P's loss of capacity, and

   (c) the person conducting the project takes in relation to P such steps as may be prescribed for the purpose of protecting him.

(3) The regulations may, in particular, –

   (a) make provision about when, for the purposes of the regulations, a project is to be treated as having begun;

   (b) include provision similar to any made by section 31, 32 or 33.

Independent mental capacity advocate service

35 Appointment of independent mental capacity advocates

(1) The appropriate authority must make such arrangements as it considers reasonable to enable persons ('independent mental capacity advocates') to be available to represent and support persons to whom acts or decisions proposed under sections 37, 38 and 39 relate.

(2) The appropriate authority may make regulations as to the appointment of independent mental capacity advocates.

(3) The regulations may, in particular, provide –

   (a) that a person may act as an independent mental capacity advocate only in such circumstances, or only subject to such conditions, as may be prescribed;

   (b) for the appointment of a person as an independent mental capacity advocate to be subject to approval in accordance with the regulations.

(4) In making arrangements under subsection (1), the appropriate authority must have regard to the principle that a person to whom a proposed act or decision relates should,

so far as practicable, be represented and supported by a person who is independent of any person who will be responsible for the act or decision.

(5) The arrangements may include provision for payments to be made to, or in relation to, persons carrying out functions in accordance with the arrangements.

(6) For the purpose of enabling him to carry out his functions, an independent mental capacity advocate –

    (a) may interview in private the person whom he has been instructed to represent, and

    (b) may, at all reasonable times, examine and take copies of –

        (i) any health record,

        (ii) any record of, or held by, a local authority and compiled in connection with a social services function, and

        (iii) any record held by a person registered under Part 2 of the Care Standards Act 2000 (c. 14),

    which the person holding the record considers may be relevant to the independent mental capacity advocate's investigation.

(7) In this section, section 36 and section 37, 'the appropriate authority' means –

    (a) in relation to the provision of the services of independent mental capacity advocates in England, the Secretary of State, and

    (b) in relation to the provision of the services of independent mental capacity advocates in Wales, the National Assembly for Wales.

36 Functions of independent mental capacity advocates

(1) The appropriate authority may make regulations as to the functions of independent mental capacity advocates.

(2) The regulations may, in particular, make provision requiring an advocate to take such steps as may be prescribed for the purpose of –

    (a) providing support to the person whom he has been instructed to represent ('P') so that P may participate as fully as possible in any relevant decision;

    (b) obtaining and evaluating relevant information;

    (c) ascertaining what P's wishes and feelings would be likely to be, and the beliefs and values that would be likely to influence P, if he had capacity;

    (d) ascertaining what alternative courses of action are available in relation to P;

    (e) obtaining a further medical opinion where treatment is proposed and the advocate thinks that one should be obtained.

(3) The regulations may also make provision as to circumstances in which the advocate may challenge, or provide assistance for the purpose of challenging, any relevant decision.

37 Provision of serious medical treatment by NHS body

(1) This section applies if an NHS body –

    (a) is proposing to provide, or secure the provision of, serious medical treatment for a person ('P') who lacks capacity to consent to the treatment, and

    (b) is satisfied that there is no person, other than one engaged in providing care or treatment for P in a professional capacity or for remuneration, whom it would be appropriate to consult in determining what would be in P's best interests.

(2) But this section does not apply if P's treatment is regulated by Part 4 of the Mental Health Act.

(3) Before the treatment is provided, the NHS body must instruct an independent mental capacity advocate to represent P.

(4) If the treatment needs to be provided as a matter of urgency, it may be provided even though the NHS body has not been able to comply with subsection (3).

(5) The NHS body must, in providing or securing the provision of treatment for P, take into account any information given, or submissions made, by the independent mental capacity advocate.

(6) 'Serious medical treatment' means treatment which involves providing, withholding or withdrawing treatment of a kind prescribed by regulations made by the appropriate authority.

(7) 'NHS body' has such meaning as may be prescribed by regulations made for the purposes of this section by –
    (a) the Secretary of State, in relation to bodies in England, or
    (b) the National Assembly for Wales, in relation to bodies in Wales.

38 Provision of accommodation by NHS body

  (1) This section applies if an NHS body proposes to make arrangements –
    (a) for the provision of accommodation in a hospital or care home for a person ('P')
      who lacks capacity to agree to the arrangements, or
    (b) for a change in P's accommodation to another hospital or care home,
and is satisfied that there is no person, other than one engaged in providing care or treatment for P in a professional capacity or for remuneration, whom it would be appropriate for it to consult in determining what would be in P's best interests.

(2) But this section does not apply if P is accommodated as a result of an obligation imposed on him under the Mental Health Act.

(3) Before making the arrangements, the NHS body must instruct an independent mental capacity advocate to represent P unless it is satisfied that –
    (a) the accommodation is likely to be provided for a continuous period which is less
      than the applicable period, or
    (b) the arrangements need to be made as a matter of urgency.

  (4) If the NHS body –
    (a) did not instruct an independent mental capacity advocate to represent P before
      making the arrangements because it was satisfied that subsection (3)(a) or (b)
      applied, but
    (b) subsequently has reason to believe that the accommodation is likely to be
      provided for a continuous period –
        (i) beginning with the day on which accommodation was first provided in
          accordance with the arrangements, and
        (ii) ending on or after the expiry of the applicable period, it must instruct an
          independent mental capacity advocate to represent P.

(5) The NHS body must, in deciding what arrangements to make for P, take into account any information given, or submissions made, by the independent mental capacity advocate.

(6) 'Care home' has the meaning given in section 3 of the Care Standards Act 2000 (c. 14).

  (7) 'Hospital' means –

(a) a health service hospital as defined by section 128 of the National Health Service Act 1977 (c. 49), or

(b) an independent hospital as defined by section 2 of the Care Standards Act 2000.

(8) 'NHS body' has such meaning as may be prescribed by regulations made for the purposes of this section by –

(a) the Secretary of State, in relation to bodies in England, or

(b) the National Assembly for Wales, in relation to bodies in Wales.

(9) 'Applicable period' means –

(a) in relation to accommodation in a hospital, 28 days, and

(b) in relation to accommodation in a care home, 8 weeks.

39 Provision of accommodation by local authority

(1) This section applies if a local authority propose to make arrangements –

(a) for the provision of residential accommodation for a person ('P') who lacks capacity to agree to the arrangements, or

(b) for a change in P's residential accommodation,

and are satisfied that there is no person, other than one engaged in providing care or treatment for P in a professional capacity or for remuneration, whom it would be appropriate for them to consult in determining what would be in P's best interests.

(2) But this section applies only if the accommodation is to be provided in accordance with –

(a) section 21 or 29 of the National Assistance Act 1948 (c. 29), or

(b) section 117 of the Mental Health Act,

as the result of a decision taken by the local authority under section 47 of the National Health Service and Community Care Act 1990 (c. 19).

(3) This section does not apply if P is accommodated as a result of an obligation imposed on him under the Mental Health Act.

(4) Before making the arrangements, the local authority must instruct an independent mental capacity advocate to represent P unless they are satisfied that –

(a) the accommodation is likely to be provided for a continuous period of less than 8 weeks, or

(b) the arrangements need to be made as a matter of urgency.

(5) If the local authority –

(a) did not instruct an independent mental capacity advocate to represent P before making the arrangements because they were satisfied that subsection (4)(a) or (b) applied, but

(b) subsequently have reason to believe that the accommodation is likely to be provided for a continuous period that will end 8 weeks or more after the day on which accommodation was first provided in accordance with the arrangements, they must instruct an independent mental capacity advocate to represent P.

(6) The local authority must, in deciding what arrangements to make for P, take into account any information given, or submissions made, by the independent mental capacity advocate.

40 Exceptions

Sections 37(3), 38(3) and (4) and 39(4) and (5) do not apply if there is –

(a) a person nominated by P (in whatever manner) as a person to be consulted in matters affecting his interests,

(b) a donee of a lasting power of attorney created by P,

(c) a deputy appointed by the court for P, or

(d) a donee of an enduring power of attorney (within the meaning of Schedule 4) created by P.

41 Power to adjust role of independent mental capacity advocate

(1) The appropriate authority may make regulations –

(a) expanding the role of independent mental capacity advocates in relation to persons who lack capacity, and

(b) adjusting the obligation to make arrangements imposed by section 35.

(2) The regulations may, in particular –

(a) prescribe circumstances (different to those set out in sections 37, 38 and 39) in which an independent mental capacity advocate must, or circumstances in which one may, be instructed by a person of a prescribed description to represent a person who lacks capacity, and

(b) include provision similar to any made by section 37, 38, 39 or 40.

(3) 'Appropriate authority' has the same meaning as in section 35.

Miscellaneous and supplementary

42 Codes of practice

(1) The Lord Chancellor must prepare and issue one or more codes of practice –

(a) for the guidance of persons assessing whether a person has capacity in relation to any matter,

(b) for the guidance of persons acting in connection with the care or treatment of another person (see section 5),

(c) for the guidance of donees of lasting powers of attorney,

(d) for the guidance of deputies appointed by the court,

(e) for the guidance of persons carrying out research in reliance on any provision made by or under this Act (and otherwise with respect to sections 30 to 34),

(f) for the guidance of independent mental capacity advocates,

(g) with respect to the provisions of sections 24 to 26 (advance decisions and apparent advance decisions), and

(h) with respect to such other matters concerned with this Act as he thinks fit.

(2) The Lord Chancellor may from time to time revise a code.

(3) The Lord Chancellor may delegate the preparation or revision of the whole or any part of a code so far as he considers expedient.

(4) It is the duty of a person to have regard to any relevant code if he is acting in relation to a person who lacks capacity and is doing so in one or more of the following ways –

(a) as the donee of a lasting power of attorney,

(b) as a deputy appointed by the court,

(c) as a person carrying out research in reliance on any provision made by or under this Act (see sections 30 to 34),

(d) as an independent mental capacity advocate,

(e) in a professional capacity,

(f) for remuneration.

(5) If it appears to a court or tribunal conducting any criminal or civil proceedings that –

(a) a provision of a code, or

(b) a failure to comply with a code,

is relevant to a question arising in the proceedings, the provision or failure must be taken into account in deciding the question.

(6) A code under subsection (1)(d) may contain separate guidance for deputies appointed by virtue of paragraph 1(2) of Schedule 5 (functions of deputy conferred on receiver appointed under the Mental Health Act).

(7) In this section and in section 43, 'code' means a code prepared or revised under this section.

43   Codes of practice: procedure

(1) Before preparing or revising a code, the Lord Chancellor must consult –

(a) the National Assembly for Wales, and

(b) such other persons as he considers appropriate.

(2) The Lord Chancellor may not issue a code unless –

(a) a draft of the code has been laid by him before both Houses of Parliament, and

(b) the 40 day period has elapsed without either House resolving not to approve the draft.

(3) The Lord Chancellor must arrange for any code that he has issued to be published in such a way as he considers appropriate for bringing it to the attention of persons likely to be concerned with its provisions.

(4) '40 day period', in relation to the draft of a proposed code, means –

(a) if the draft is laid before one House on a day later than the day on which it is laid before the other House, the period of 40 days beginning with the later of the two days;

(b) in any other case, the period of 40 days beginning with the day on which it is laid before each House.

(5) In calculating the period of 40 days, no account is to be taken of any period during which Parliament is dissolved or prorogued or during which both Houses are adjourned for more than 4 days.

44   Ill-treatment or neglect

(1) Subsection (2) applies if a person ('D') –

(a) has the care of a person ('P') who lacks, or whom D reasonably believes to lack, capacity,

(b) is the donee of a lasting power of attorney, or an enduring power of attorney (within the meaning of Schedule 4), created by P, or

(c) is a deputy appointed by the court for P.

(2) D is guilty of an offence if he ill-treats or wilfully neglects P.

(3) A person guilty of an offence under this section is liable –

    (a) on summary conviction, to imprisonment for a term not exceeding 12 months or a fine not exceeding the statutory maximum or both;

    (b) on conviction on indictment, to imprisonment for a term not exceeding 5 years or a fine or both.

Part 2   The Court of Protection and the Public Guardian

The Court of Protection

45   The Court of Protection

(1) There is to be a superior court of record known as the Court of Protection.

(2) The court is to have an official seal.

(3) The court may sit at any place in England and Wales, on any day and at any time.

(4) The court is to have a central office and registry at a place appointed by the Lord Chancellor.

(5) The Lord Chancellor may designate as additional registries of the court any district registry of the High Court and any county court office.

(6) The office of the Supreme Court called the Court of Protection ceases to exist.

46   The judges of the Court of Protection

(1) Subject to Court of Protection Rules under section 51(2)(d), the jurisdiction of the court is exercisable by a judge nominated for that purpose by –

    (a) the Lord Chancellor, or

    (b) a person acting on the Lord Chancellor's behalf.

(2) To be nominated, a judge must be –

    (a) the President of the Family Division,

    (b) the Vice-Chancellor,

    (c) a puisne judge of the High Court,

    (d) a circuit judge, or

    (e) a district judge.

(3) The Lord Chancellor must –

    (a) appoint one of the judges nominated by virtue of subsection (2)(a) to (c) to be President of the Court of Protection, and

    (b) appoint another of those judges to be Vice-President of the Court of Protection.

(4) The Lord Chancellor must appoint one of the judges nominated by virtue of subsection (2)(d) or (e) to be Senior Judge of the Court of Protection, having such administrative functions in relation to the court as the Lord Chancellor may direct.

Supplementary powers

47   General powers and effect of orders etc.

(1) The court has in connection with its jurisdiction the same powers, rights, privileges and authority as the High Court.

(2) Section 204 of the Law of Property Act 1925 (c. 20) (orders of High Court conclusive in favour of purchasers) applies in relation to orders and directions of the court as it applies to orders of the High Court.

(3) Office copies of orders made, directions given or other instruments issued by the court and sealed with its official seal are admissible in all legal proceedings as evidence of the originals without any further proof.

48 Interim orders and directions

The court may, pending the determination of an application to it in relation to a person ('P'), make an order or give directions in respect of any matter if –

    (a) there is reason to believe that P lacks capacity in relation to the matter,

    (b) the matter is one to which its powers under this Act extend, and

    (c) it is in P's best interests to make the order, or give the directions, without delay.

49 Power to call for reports

(1) This section applies where, in proceedings brought in respect of a person ('P') under Part 1, the court is considering a question relating to P.

(2) The court may require a report to be made to it by the Public Guardian or by a Court of Protection Visitor.

(3) The court may require a local authority, or an NHS body, to arrange for a report to be made –

    (a) by one of its officers or employees, or

    (b) by such other person (other than the Public Guardian or a Court of Protection Visitor) as the authority, or the NHS body, considers appropriate.

(4) The report must deal with such matters relating to P as the court may direct.

(5) Court of Protection Rules may specify matters which, unless the court directs otherwise, must also be dealt with in the report.

(6) The report may be made in writing or orally, as the court may direct.

(7) In complying with a requirement, the Public Guardian or a Court of Protection Visitor may, at all reasonable times, examine and take copies of –

    (a) any health record,

    (b) any record of, or held by, a local authority and compiled in connection with a social services function, and

    (c) any record held by a person registered under Part 2 of the Care Standards Act 2000 (c. 14),

so far as the record relates to P.

(8) If the Public Guardian or a Court of Protection Visitor is making a visit in the course of complying with a requirement, he may interview P in private.

(9) If a Court of Protection Visitor who is a Special Visitor is making a visit in the course of complying with a requirement, he may if the court so directs carry out in private a medical, psychiatric or psychological examination of P's capacity and condition.

(10) 'NHS body' has the meaning given in section 148 of the Health and Social Care (Community Health and Standards) Act 2003 (c. 43).

(11) 'Requirement' means a requirement imposed under subsection (2) or (3).

Practice and procedure

50 Applications to the Court of Protection

(1) No permission is required for an application to the court for the exercise of any of its powers under this Act –

    (a) by a person who lacks, or is alleged to lack, capacity,

    (b) if such a person has not reached 18, by anyone with parental responsibility for him,

    (c) by the donor or a donee of a lasting power of attorney to which the application relates,

    (d) by a deputy appointed by the court for a person to whom the application relates, or

    (e) by a person named in an existing order of the court, if the application relates to the order.

(2) But, subject to Court of Protection Rules and to paragraph 20(2) of Schedule 3 (declarations relating to private international law), permission is required for any other application to the court.

(3) In deciding whether to grant permission the court must, in particular, have regard to –

    (a) the applicant's connection with the person to whom the application relates,

    (b) the reasons for the application,

    (c) the benefit to the person to whom the application relates of a proposed order or directions, and

    (d) whether the benefit can be achieved in any other way.

(4) 'Parental responsibility' has the same meaning as in the Children Act 1989 (c. 41).

51 Court of Protection Rules

(1) The Lord Chancellor may make rules of court (to be called 'Court of Protection Rules') with respect to the practice and procedure of the court.

(2) Court of Protection Rules may, in particular, make provision –

    (a) as to the manner and form in which proceedings are to be commenced;

    (b) as to the persons entitled to be notified of, and be made parties to, the proceedings;

    (c) for the allocation, in such circumstances as may be specified, of any specified description of proceedings to a specified judge or to specified descriptions of judges;

    (d) for the exercise of the jurisdiction of the court, in such circumstances as may be specified, by its officers or other staff;

    (e) for enabling the court to appoint a suitable person (who may, with his consent, be the Official Solicitor) to act in the name of, or on behalf of, or to represent the person to whom the proceedings relate;

    (f) for enabling an application to the court to be disposed of without a hearing;

    (g) for enabling the court to proceed with, or with any part of, a hearing in the absence of the person to whom the proceedings relate;

    (h) for enabling or requiring the proceedings or any part of them to be conducted in private and for enabling the court to determine who is to be admitted when the court sits in private and to exclude specified persons when it sits in public;

> (i) as to what may be received as evidence (whether or not admissible apart from the rules) and the manner in which it is to be presented;
>
> (j) for the enforcement of orders made and directions given in the proceedings.

(3) Court of Protection Rules may, instead of providing for any matter, refer to provision made or to be made about that matter by directions.

(4) Court of Protection Rules may make different provision for different areas.

52 Practice directions

(1) The President of the Court of Protection may, with the concurrence of the Lord Chancellor, give directions as to the practice and procedure of the court.

(2) Directions as to the practice and procedure of the court may not be given by anyone other than the President of the Court of Protection without the approval of the President of the Court of Protection and the Lord Chancellor.

(3) Nothing in this section prevents the President of the Court of Protection, without the concurrence of the Lord Chancellor, giving directions which contain guidance as to law or making judicial decisions.

53 Rights of appeal

(1) Subject to the provisions of this section, an appeal lies to the Court of Appeal from any decision of the court.

(2) Court of Protection Rules may provide that where a decision of the court is made by –

> (a) a person exercising the jurisdiction of the court by virtue of rules made under section 51(2)(d),
>
> (b) a district judge, or
>
> (c) a circuit judge,

an appeal from that decision lies to a prescribed higher judge of the court and not to the Court of Appeal.

(3) For the purposes of this section the higher judges of the court are –

> (a) in relation to a person mentioned in subsection (2)(a), a circuit judge or a district judge;
>
> (b) in relation to a person mentioned in subsection (2)(b), a circuit judge;
>
> (c) in relation to any person mentioned in subsection (2), one of the judges nominated by virtue of section 46(2)(a) to (c).

(4) Court of Protection Rules may make provision –

> (a) that, in such cases as may be specified, an appeal from a decision of the court may not be made without permission;
>
> (b) as to the person or persons entitled to grant permission to appeal;
>
> (c) as to any requirements to be satisfied before permission is granted;
>
> (d) that where a higher judge of the court makes a decision on an appeal, no appeal may be made to the Court of Appeal from that decision unless the Court of Appeal considers that –
>
> > (i) the appeal would raise an important point of principle or practice, or
> >
> > (ii) there is some other compelling reason for the Court of Appeal to hear it;
>
> (e) as to any considerations to be taken into account in relation to granting or refusing permission to appeal.

Fees and costs

54 Fees

(1) The Lord Chancellor may with the consent of the Treasury by order prescribe fees payable in respect of anything dealt with by the court.

(2) An order under this section may in particular contain provision as to –

(a) scales or rates of fees;

(b) exemptions from and reductions in fees;

(c) remission of fees in whole or in part.

(3) Before making an order under this section, the Lord Chancellor must consult –

(a) the President of the Court of Protection,

(b) the Vice-President of the Court of Protection, and

(c) the Senior Judge of the Court of Protection.

(4) The Lord Chancellor must take such steps as are reasonably practicable to bring information about fees to the attention of persons likely to have to pay them.

(5) Fees payable under this section are recoverable summarily as a civil debt.

55 Costs

(1) Subject to Court of Protection Rules, the costs of and incidental to all proceedings in the court are in its discretion.

(2) The rules may in particular make provision for regulating matters relating to the costs of those proceedings, including prescribing scales of costs to be paid to legal or other representatives.

(3) The court has full power to determine by whom and to what extent the costs are to be paid.

(4) The court may, in any proceedings –

(a) disallow, or

(b) order the legal or other representatives concerned to meet,

the whole of any wasted costs or such part of them as may be determined in accordance with the rules.

(5) 'Legal or other representative', in relation to a party to proceedings, means any person exercising a right of audience or right to conduct litigation on his behalf.

(6) 'Wasted costs' means any costs incurred by a party –

(a) as a result of any improper, unreasonable or negligent act or omission on the part of any legal or other representative or any employee of such a representative, or

(b) which, in the light of any such act or omission occurring after they were incurred, the court considers it is unreasonable to expect that party to pay.

56 Fees and costs: supplementary

(1) Court of Protection Rules may make provision –

(a) as to the way in which, and funds from which, fees and costs are to be paid;

(b) for charging fees and costs upon the estate of the person to whom the proceedings relate;

(c) for the payment of fees and costs within a specified time of the death of the person to whom the proceedings relate or the conclusion of the proceedings.

(2) A charge on the estate of a person created by virtue of subsection (1)(b) does not cause any interest of the person in any property to fail or determine or to be prevented from recommencing.

The Public Guardian

57 The Public Guardian

(1) For the purposes of this Act, there is to be an officer, to be known as the Public Guardian.

(2) The Public Guardian is to be appointed by the Lord Chancellor.

(3) There is to be paid to the Public Guardian out of money provided by Parliament such salary as the Lord Chancellor may determine.

(4) The Lord Chancellor may, after consulting the Public Guardian –

    (a) provide him with such officers and staff, or

    (b) enter into such contracts with other persons for the provision (by them or their sub-contractors) of officers, staff or services,

as the Lord Chancellor thinks necessary for the proper discharge of the Public Guardian's functions.

(5) Any functions of the Public Guardian may, to the extent authorised by him, be performed by any of his officers.

58 Functions of the Public Guardian

(1) The Public Guardian has the following functions –

    (a) establishing and maintaining a register of lasting powers of attorney,

    (b) establishing and maintaining a register of orders appointing deputies,

    (c) supervising deputies appointed by the court,

    (d) directing a Court of Protection Visitor to visit –

        (i) a donee of a lasting power of attorney,

        (ii) a deputy appointed by the court, or

        (iii) the person granting the power of attorney or for whom the deputy is appointed ('P'),

and to make a report to the Public Guardian on such matters as he may direct,

    (e) receiving security which the court requires a person to give for the discharge of his functions,

    (f) receiving reports from donees of lasting powers of attorney and deputies appointed by the court,

    (g) reporting to the court on such matters relating to proceedings under this Act as the court requires,

    (h) dealing with representations (including complaints) about the way in which a donee of a lasting power of attorney or a deputy appointed by the court is exercising his powers,

    (i) publishing, in any manner the Public Guardian thinks appropriate, any information he thinks appropriate about the discharge of his functions.

(2) The functions conferred by subsection (1)(c) and (h) may be discharged in co-operation with any other person who has functions in relation to the care or treatment of P.

(3) The Lord Chancellor may by regulations make provision –

    (a) conferring on the Public Guardian other functions in connection with this Act;

(b) in connection with the discharge by the Public Guardian of his functions.

(4) Regulations made under subsection (3)(b) may in particular make provision as to –

(a) the giving of security by deputies appointed by the court and the enforcement and discharge of security so given;

(b) the fees which may be charged by the Public Guardian;

(c) the way in which, and funds from which, such fees are to be paid;

(d) exemptions from and reductions in such fees;

(e) remission of such fees in whole or in part;

(f) the making of reports to the Public Guardian by deputies appointed by the court and others who are directed by the court to carry out any transaction for a person who lacks capacity.

(5) For the purpose of enabling him to carry out his functions, the Public Guardian may, at all reasonable times, examine and take copies of –

(a) any health record,

(b) any record of, or held by, a local authority and compiled in connection with a social services function, and

(c) any record held by a person registered under Part 2 of the Care Standards Act 2000 (c. 14),

so far as the record relates to P.

(6) The Public Guardian may also for that purpose interview P in private.

59 Public Guardian Board

(1) There is to be a body, to be known as the Public Guardian Board.

(2) The Board's duty is to scrutinise and review the way in which the Public Guardian discharges his functions and to make such recommendations to the Lord Chancellor about that matter as it thinks appropriate.

(3) The Lord Chancellor must, in discharging his functions under sections 57 and 58, give due consideration to recommendations made by the Board.

(4) The members of the Board are to be appointed by the Lord Chancellor.

(5) The Board must have –

(a) at least one member who is a judge of the court, and

(b) at least four members who are persons appearing to the Lord Chancellor to have appropriate knowledge or experience of the work of the Public Guardian.

(6) The Lord Chancellor may by regulations make provision as to –

(a) the appointment of members of the Board (and, in particular, the procedures to be followed in connection with appointments);

(b) the selection of one of the members to be the chairman;

(c) the term of office of the chairman and members;

(d) their resignation, suspension or removal;

(e) the procedure of the Board (including quorum);

(f) the validation of proceedings in the event of a vacancy among the members or a defect in the appointment of a member.

(7) Subject to any provision made in reliance on subsection (6)(c) or (d), a person is to hold and vacate office as a member of the Board in accordance with the terms of the instrument appointing him.

(8) The Lord Chancellor may make such payments to or in respect of members of the Board by way of reimbursement of expenses, allowances and remuneration as he may determine.

(9) The Board must make an annual report to the Lord Chancellor about the discharge of its functions.

60   Annual report

(1) The Public Guardian must make an annual report to the Lord Chancellor about the discharge of his functions.

(2) The Lord Chancellor must, within one month of receiving the report, lay a copy of it before Parliament.

Court of Protection Visitors

61   Court of Protection Visitors

(1) A Court of Protection Visitor is a person who is appointed by the Lord Chancellor to –
    (a) a panel of Special Visitors, or
    (b) a panel of General Visitors.

(2) A person is not qualified to be a Special Visitor unless he –
    (a) is a registered medical practitioner or appears to the Lord Chancellor to have other suitable qualifications or training, and
    (b) appears to the Lord Chancellor to have special knowledge of and experience in cases of impairment of or disturbance in the functioning of the mind or brain.

(3) A General Visitor need not have a medical qualification.

(4) A Court of Protection Visitor –
    (a) may be appointed for such term and subject to such conditions, and
    (b) may be paid such remuneration and allowances,
as the Lord Chancellor may determine.

(5) For the purpose of carrying out his functions under this Act in relation to a person who lacks capacity ('P'), a Court of Protection Visitor may, at all reasonable times, examine and take copies of –
    (a) any health record,
    (b) any record of, or held by, a local authority and compiled in connection with a social services function, and
    (c) any record held by a person registered under Part 2 of the Care Standards Act 2000 (c. 14),
so far as the record relates to P.

(6) A Court of Protection Visitor may also for that purpose interview P in private.

Part 3   Miscellaneous and general

Declaratory provision

62   Scope of the Act

For the avoidance of doubt, it is hereby declared that nothing in this Act is to be taken to affect the law relating to murder or manslaughter or the operation of section 2 of the Suicide Act 1961 (c. 60) (assisting suicide).

Private international law

63 International protection of adults

Schedule 3 –

    (a) gives effect in England and Wales to the Convention on the International Protection of Adults signed at the Hague on 13th January 2000 (Cm. 5881) (in so far as this Act does not otherwise do so), and

    (b) makes related provision as to the private international law of England and Wales.

General

64 Interpretation

(1) In this Act –

'the 1985 Act' means the Enduring Powers of Attorney Act 1985 (c. 29),

'advance decision' has the meaning given in section 24(1),

'the court' means the Court of Protection established by section 45,

'Court of Protection Rules' has the meaning given in section 51(1),

'Court of Protection Visitor' has the meaning given in section 61,

'deputy' has the meaning given in section 16(2)(b),

'enactment' includes a provision of subordinate legislation (within the meaning of the Interpretation Act 1978 (c. 30)),

'health record' has the meaning given in section 68 of the Data Protection Act 1998 (c. 29) (as read with section 69 of that Act),

'the Human Rights Convention' has the same meaning as 'the Convention' in the Human Rights Act 1998 (c. 42),

'independent mental capacity advocate' has the meaning given in section 35(1),

'lasting power of attorney' has the meaning given in section 9,

'life-sustaining treatment' has the meaning given in section 4(10),

'local authority' means –

    (a) the council of a county in England in which there are no district councils,

    (b) the council of a district in England,

    (c) the council of a county or county borough in Wales,

    (d) the council of a London borough,

    (e) the Common Council of the City of London, or

    (f) the Council of the Isles of Scilly,

'Mental Health Act' means the Mental Health Act 1983 (c. 20),

'prescribed', in relation to regulations made under this Act, means prescribed by those regulations,

'property' includes any thing in action and any interest in real or personal property,

'public authority' has the same meaning as in the Human Rights Act 1998,

'Public Guardian' has the meaning given in section 57,

'purchaser' and 'purchase' have the meaning given in section 205(1) of the Law of Property Act 1925 (c. 20),

'social services function' has the meaning given in section 1A of the Local Authority Social Services Act 1970 (c. 42),

'treatment' includes a diagnostic or other procedure,

'trust corporation' has the meaning given in section 68(1) of the Trustee Act 1925 (c. 19), and

'will' includes codicil.

(2) In this Act, references to making decisions, in relation to a donee of a lasting power of attorney or a deputy appointed by the court, include, where appropriate, acting on decisions made.

(3) In this Act, references to the bankruptcy of an individual include a case where a bankruptcy restrictions order under the Insolvency Act 1986 (c. 45) has effect in respect of him.

(4) 'Bankruptcy restrictions order' includes an interim bankruptcy restrictions order.

65 Rules, regulations and orders

(1) Any power to make rules, regulations or orders under this Act –
   (a) is exercisable by statutory instrument;
   (b) includes power to make supplementary, incidental, consequential, transitional or saving provision;
   (c) includes power to make different provision for different cases.

(2) Any statutory instrument containing rules, regulations or orders made by the Lord Chancellor or the Secretary of State under this Act, other than –
   (a) regulations under section 34 (loss of capacity during research project),
   (b) regulations under section 41 (adjusting role of independent mental capacity advocacy service),
   (c) regulations under paragraph 32(1)(b) of Schedule 3 (private international law relating to the protection of adults),
   (d) an order of the kind mentioned in section 67(6) (consequential amendments of primary legislation), or
   (e) an order under section 68 (commencement),

is subject to annulment in pursuance of a resolution of either House of Parliament.

(3) A statutory instrument containing an Order in Council under paragraph 31 of Schedule 3 (provision to give further effect to Hague Convention) is subject to annulment in pursuance of a resolution of either House of Parliament.

(4) A statutory instrument containing regulations made by the Secretary of State under section 34 or 41 or by the Lord Chancellor under paragraph 32(1)(b) of Schedule 3 may not be made unless a draft has been laid before and approved by resolution of each House of Parliament.

66 Existing receivers and enduring powers of attorney etc.

(1) The following provisions cease to have effect –
   (a) Part 7 of the Mental Health Act,
   (b) the Enduring Powers of Attorney Act 1985 (c. 29).

(2) No enduring power of attorney within the meaning of the 1985 Act is to be created after the commencement of subsection (1)(b).

(3) Schedule 4 has effect in place of the 1985 Act in relation to any enduring power of attorney created before the commencement of subsection (1)(b).

(4) Schedule 5 contains transitional provisions and savings in relation to Part 7 of the Mental Health Act and the 1985 Act.

67   Minor and consequential amendments and repeals

(1) Schedule 6 contains minor and consequential amendments.

(2) Schedule 7 contains repeals.

(3) The Lord Chancellor may by order make supplementary, incidental, consequential, transitional or saving provision for the purposes of, in consequence of, or for giving full effect to a provision of this Act.

(4) An order under subsection (3) may, in particular –

> (a) provide for a provision of this Act which comes into force before another provision of this Act has come into force to have effect, until the other provision has come into force, with specified modifications;
>
> (b) amend, repeal or revoke an enactment, other than one contained in an Act or Measure passed in a Session after the one in which this Act is passed.

(5) The amendments that may be made under subsection (4)(b) are in addition to those made by or under any other provision of this Act.

(6) An order under subsection (3) which amends or repeals a provision of an Act or Measure may not be made unless a draft has been laid before and approved by resolution of each House of Parliament.

68   Commencement and extent

(1) This Act, other than sections 30 to 41, comes into force in accordance with provision made by order by the Lord Chancellor.

(2) Sections 30 to 41 come into force in accordance with provision made by order by –

> (a) the Secretary of State, in relation to England, and
>
> (b) the National Assembly for Wales, in relation to Wales.

(3) An order under this section may appoint different days for different provisions and different purposes.

(4) Subject to subsections (5) and (6), this Act extends to England and Wales only.

(5) The following provisions extend to the United Kingdom –

> (a) paragraph 16(1) of Schedule 1 (evidence of instruments and of registration of lasting powers of attorney),
>
> (b) paragraph 15(3) of Schedule 4 (evidence of instruments and of registration of enduring powers of attorney).

(6) Subject to any provision made in Schedule 6, the amendments and repeals made by Schedules 6 and 7 have the same extent as the enactments to which they relate.

69   Short title

This Act may be cited as the Mental Capacity Act 2005.

Appendix 2 Helping people to make their own decisions

2.A A quick summary as set out in Chapter 3 of the Code of Practice to the Mental Capacity Act 2005

To help someone make a decision for themselves, check the following points:

Providing relevant information

- Does the person have all the relevant information they need to make a particular decision?
- If they have a choice, have they been given information on all the alternatives?

Communicating in an appropriate way

- Could information be explained or presented in a way that is easier for the person to understand (for example, by using simple language or visual aids)?
- Have different methods of communication been explored if required, including non-verbal communication?
- Could anyone else help with communication (for example, a family member, support worker, interpreter, speech and language therapist or advocate)?

Making the person feel at ease

- Are there particular times of day when the person's understanding is better?
- Are there particular locations where they may feel more at ease?
- Could the decision be put off to see whether the person can make the decision at a later time when circumstances are right for them?

Supporting the person

- Can anyone else help or support the person to make choices or express a view?

2B

If the person is still unable to make the decision and you have to act under s 5:

Key checks for decision-makers

1. What is the act or decision?
2. Why does it need to be performed now?
3. Do you have a reasonable belief that the person lacks capacity in relation to the matter at the particular time of intervention (see Appendix 3)? And finally
4. Can you confirm that it will be in the person's best interests and that you have followed the checklist (see Appendix 4).

Appendix 3 Assessing capacity

The quick summary at the beginning of Chapter 4 of the Code of Practice provides a useful checklist.

Assessing capacity

This checklist is a summary of points to consider when assessing a person's capacity to make a specific decision:

Presuming someone has capacity

- The starting assumption must always be that a person has the capacity to make a decision, unless it can be established that they lack capacity.

Understanding what is meant by capacity and lack of capacity

- A person's capacity must be assessed specifically in terms of their capacity to make a particular decision at the time it needs to be made.

Treating everyone equally

- A person's capacity must not be judged simply on the basis of their age, appearance, condition or an aspect of their behaviour.

Supporting the person to make the decision for themselves

- It is important to take all possible steps to try to help people make a decision for themselves.

Assessing capacity

- Anyone assessing someone's capacity to make a decision for themselves should use the two-stage test of capacity.
- Does the person have an impairment of the mind or brain, or is there some sort of disturbance affecting the way their brain or mind works? (It doesn't matter whether the impairment or disturbance is temporary or permanent.)
- If so, does that impairment or disturbance mean that the person is unable to make the decision in question at the time it needs to be made?

Assessing ability to make a decision

- Does the person have a general understanding of what decision they need to make and why they need to make it?

- Does the person have a general understanding of the likely consequences of making, or not making, this decision?
- Is the person able to understand, retain, use and weigh up the information relevant to this decision?
- Can the person communicate their decision (by talking, using sign language or any other means)? Would the services of a professional (such as a speech and language therapist) be helpful?

Assessing capacity to make more complex or serious decisions

- Is there a need for a more thorough assessment (perhaps by involving a doctor or other professional expert)?

Appendix 4 Best interests checklist

From the quick summary in Chapter 5 of the Code of Practice to the Mental Capacity Act 2005

A person trying to work out the best interests of a person who lacks capacity to make a particular decision ('lacks capacity') should:

Encourage participation

- Do whatever is possible to permit and encourage the person to take part, or to improve their ability to take part, in making the decision.

Identify all relevant circumstances

- Try to identify all the things that the person who lacks capacity would take into account if they were making the decision or acting for themselves

Find out the person's views

- Try to find out the views of the person who lacks capacity, including:
  - the person's past and present wishes and feelings – these may have been expressed verbally, in writing or through behaviour or habits
  - any beliefs and values (e.g. religious, cultural, moral or political) that would be likely to influence the decision in question
  - any other factors the person themselves would be likely to consider if they were making the decision or acting for themselves.

Avoid discrimination

- Not make assumptions about someone's best interests simply on the basis of the person's age, appearance, condition or behaviour.

Assess whether the person might regain capacity

- Consider whether the person is likely to regain capacity (e.g. after receiving medical treatment). If so, can the decision wait until then?

If the decision concerns life-sustaining treatment

- Not be motivated in any way by a desire to bring about the person's death. They should not make assumptions about the person's quality of life.

Consult others

- If it is practical and appropriate to do so, consult other people for their views about the person's best interests and to see if they have any information about the person's wishes and feelings, beliefs and values. In particular, try to consult:
  - anyone previously named by the person as someone to be consulted on either the decision in question or on similar issues
  - anyone engaged in caring for the person
  - close relatives, friends or others who take an interest in the person's welfare
  - any attorney appointed under a Lasting Power of Attorney or Enduring Power of Attorney made by the person
  - any deputy appointed by the Court of Protection to make decisions for the person.
- For decisions about major medical treatment or where the person should live and where there is no-one who fits into any of the above categories, an Independent Mental Capacity Advocate (IMCA) must be consulted. (see Code, Chapter 10 for more information about IMCAs).
- When consulting, remember that the person who lacks the capacity to make the decision or act for themselves still has a right to keep their affairs private – so it would not be right to share every piece of information with everyone.

Avoid restricting the person's rights

- see if there are other options that may be less restrictive of the person's rights.

Take all of this into account

- weigh up all of these factors in order to work out what is in the person's best interests

Appendix 5   Multiple choice answers

This appendix gives the answers to the questions that appear at the end of some chapters. The first number gives the chapter number, so 2.1 is the first question at the end of Chapter 2. If the reasons for the answers are not clear, return to the body of the chapter for an explanation.

2.1   The Mental Capacity Act 2005:
  (a) Places advance decisions relating to treatment on a statutory footing ✓
  (b) Defines incapacity ✓
  (c) Retains the current common law test for capacity to consent to treatment, without change ☐
  (d) Introduces substituted decision-making in relation to healthcare matters ✓
  (e) Regulates research relating to incapacitated persons ✓
  (f) Fills the 'Bournewood gap' by allowing deputies to authorise deprivation of liberty ☐

2.2   The Mental Capacity Act contains a checklist which determines who should be the decision-maker in any specified situation:
  (a) True ☐
  (b) False ✓

2.3   Under the Mental Capacity Act someone may be appointed under a Lasting Power of Attorney to make healthcare decisions for a person when he/she becomes incapacitated:
  (a) True ✓
  (b) False ☐

2.4   To be protected when doing anything under s 5 of the Act a person must:
  (a) establish that the person lacks capacity in relation to the matter in question ☐
  (b) notify the Public Guardian of the decision if it incurs significant costs ☐
  (c) believe that the action will be in the person's best interests ☐
  (d) obtain medical evidence of mental incapacity ☐
  (e) inform the nearest relative of any action taken ☐

3.1   The Code of Practice to the Mental Capacity Act 2005 provides guidance for:
  (a) people assessing capacity ✓
  (b) people appointed as attorneys under Lasting Powers of Attorney ✓
  (c) people appointed as guardians under the Mental Health Act 1983 ☐

(d) deputies appointed by the Court of Protection ✓

(e) Independent Mental Capacity Advocates ✓

(f) Independent Mental Health Advocates ☐

3.2 Under the Mental Capacity Act a failure to follow the Code of Practice would always lead to court proceedings if reported to the relevant authority:

(a) True ☐

(b) False ✓

3.3 Principles for the Mental Capacity Act are set out in the Code of Practice and not in the Act itself:

(a) True ☐

(b) False ✓

4.1 Key principles of the Mental Capacity Act include:

(a) A presumption of capacity exists for all those aged 16 or over ✓

(b) All practicable steps are to be taken to help a person make the decision before they're considered incapable ✓

(c) An unwise decision implies a lack of capacity ☐

(d) Acts done on behalf of an incapacitated person must be in his/her best interests ✓

(e) All decisions made on behalf of an incapacitated person must be registered with the Court of Protection ☐

(f) Decisions should be the least expensive available in terms of cost to the person ☐

(g) Decisions should seek to be less restrictive in terms of the person's rights and freedom of action ✓

4.2 The Court of Protection is not covered by the principles as they only apply to other decision-makers under the Act:

(a) True ☐

(b) False ✓

5.1 A decision on a person's mental capacity needs to be made in relation to the particular matter at the time when the decision has to be made:

(a) True ✓

(b) False ☐

5.2 The test for capacity under the Mental Capacity Act is whether the person can:

(a) Understand the relevant information ✓

(b) Retain the relevant information ✓

(c) Believe the relevant information ☐

(d) Use or weigh the relevant information as part of the decision-making process ✓

(e) Communicate the decision ☑

(f) Read and sign a consent form ☐

5.3 The fact that a person is able to retain the information relevant to a decision for a short period only will prevent him from being regarded as able to make the decision:

(a) True ☐

(b) False ☑

6.1 According to the Mental Capacity Act decisions made in relation to an incapacitated person must be in that person's best interests but the list of points to consider are in the Code rather than being set out in the statute:

(a) True ☑

(b) False ☐

6.2 Following best interests could lead to the withdrawal of life-sustaining treatment:

(a) True ☑

(b) False ☐

6.3 The best interests checklist includes:

(a) Decisions should not be based on a person's appearance ☑

(b) Waiting where possible for the person to regain capacity ☑

(c) Never going against the incapacitated person's current views ☐

(d) Consulting anyone who has been named by the person ☑

(e) Seeking to incur minimal expense for the person themselves ☐

(f) Identifying all relevant circumstances ☑

11.1 The IMCA service:

(a) is based on a statutory requirement ☑

(b) uses only qualified solicitors ☐

(c) aims to represent and support people for particular acts ☑

(d) provides substituted decision-making in relation to healthcare matters ☐

(e) may be involved in vulnerable adult procedures ☑

(f) has the right to interview certain people in private ☑

11.2 IMCAs provide a form of non-instructional advocacy:

(a) True ☑

(b) False ☐

11.3 An IMCA has the power to veto any decision made by a local authority or NHS Trust:

(a) True ☐

(b) False ☑

12.1 The following would be typical situations where the Court of Protection would be involved:

    (a) it was felt that there might be the need for a deputy to be appointed ☑

    (b) a person was appealing against detention under the Mental Health Act ☐

    (c) a person wished to challenge a decision that he lacked capacity in relation to a matter ☑

    (d) a nearest relative wanted to make an application for guardianship ☐

    (e) someone alleged that an attorney was not applying the best interests checklist ☑

    (f) an IMCA believed a decision-maker was failing to take into account his submissions as to what was in the best interests of a person lacking capacity ☑

12.2 The Court of Protection can only intervene if the person in question has a mental disorder as defined by the Mental Health Act 1983:

    (a) True ☐

    (b) False ☑

12.3 The Public Guardian is responsible for:

    (a) establishing and maintaining registers of LPAs ☑

    (b) establishing and maintaining registers of guardianships under the Mental Health Act ☐

    (c) supervising court-appointed deputies ☑

    (d) supervising nearest relatives appointed by the County Court ☐

    (e) directing Court of Protection Visitors to visit and report on persons lacking capacity ☑

    (f) receiving reports from deputies or attorneys ☑

15.1 'An impairment of, or a disturbance in the functioning of, the mind or brain' is a key phrase to be found in **BOTH** the Mental Health Act 2007 and the Mental Capacity Act 2005:

    (a) True ☐

    (b) False ☑

15.2 In *HL v UK* the European Court ruled that there had been breaches of:

    (a) Article 3 – prohibition of torture ☐

    (b) Article 5.1 – right to liberty and security of person ☑

    (c) Article 5.4 – right to a speedy review of detention ☑

    (d) Article 8.1 – right to respect for private and family life ☐

    (e) Article 12 – right to marry and found a family ☐

    (f) Article 14 – prohibition of discrimination ☐

15.3 The Mental Capacity Act limits the following areas to people of 18 or over:

    (a) making an advance decision ☑

    (b) any intervention under s 5 on the basis of mental incapacity ☐

(c) making a Lasting Power of Attorney ☑

(d) being a named person for consultation as part of the best interests checklist ☐

(e) becoming an attorney under a Lasting Power of Attorney ☑

(f) use of the new Bournewood safeguards when implemented ☑

16.1 The Government now plans to introduce measures to close the 'Bournewood gap'. For relevant cases supervisory bodies will commission the following assessments:

(a) Best interests ☑

(b) Objections (e.g. from LPA) ☑

(c) Age ☑

(d) Financial ☐

(e) Eligibility ☑

(f) Whether receiving MH Act s 117 after-care ☐

(g) Mental capacity ☑

(h) Abnormally aggressive or seriously irresponsible conduct ☐

(i) Mental disorder ☑

16.2 Under the new 'Bournewood' measures one professional could carry out all of the required assessments:

(a) True ☐

(b) False ☑

16.3 Under the new 'Bournewood' measures a representative will be appointed for the individual after deprivation of liberty has been authorised:

(a) True ☑

(b) False ☐

Appendix 6 Lasting Powers of Attorney and advance decisions

This appendix summarises some key points and questions relating to Lasting Powers of Attorney (LPAs) and to advance decisions. Details on the LPA points are contained in Chapter 8 and details on advance decisions are in Chapter 10.

Key points and questions relating to Lasting Powers of Attorney

- What area of decision-making does the person wish to cover?
- Does the LPA cover this area of decision-making?
- Have the formal requirements been met if the LPA covers life-sustaining treatment?
- Did the donor understand what was included in life-sustaining treatment?
- How old is the donor/attorney? They must both be at least 18.
- The LPA does not bypass best interests checklist and s 1 principles.
- Has the donor of a personal welfare LPA become incapacitated?
- Can the donor make the relevant decision for himself?
- Does the LPA cover the same ground as an advance decision?
- Is the attorney failing to act in the best interests of the donor, or abusing him?

Key points and questions relating to advance decisions

- If the advance decision is to refuse life-sustaining treatment, does it meet the formal requirements?
- Did the person have capacity when making the advance decision?
- Is there any evidence of a change of mind or of withdrawal?
- Is there a change of circumstances which may have affected the person's decision?
- Does the advance decision clearly cover the treatment in question?
- Did the person mean the advance decision to apply in these circumstances?
- If not meeting the requirements for an advance decision it may still be a statement of wishes to be considered under s 4
- An advance decision trumps the best interests checklist
- An advance decision does not cover treatment regulated by Part 4 of the Mental Health Act 1983
- Is there an LPA covering the same circumstances?

Appendix 7 Deprivation of liberty

What amounts to deprivation of liberty?

There is no single factor which determines deprivation of liberty. In the *Bournewood* case (*HL v UK*, 2004) the European Court of Human Rights stated that the difference was one of degree or intensity rather than nature or substance. It may depend on the type of care being provided, how long the situation lasts, what the effects are and how the situation came about. There is some guidance in the Code of Practice (para 6.52) as to what factors contribute to deprivation of liberty.

The European Court of Human Rights has identified the following as factors contributing to deprivation of liberty in its judgments on cases to date:

- *restraint was used, including sedation, to admit a person who is resisting*
- *professionals exercised complete and effective control over care and movement for a significant period*
- *professionals exercised control over assessments, treatment, contacts and residence*
- *the person would be prevented from leaving if they made a meaningful attempt to do so*
- *a request by carers for the person to be discharged to their care was refused*
- *the person was unable to maintain social contacts because of restrictions placed on access to other people*
- *the person lost autonomy because they were under continuous supervision and control.*

Appendix 8 The new 'Bournewood' proposals

When these changes to the Mental Capacity Act 2005 are implemented, the managing authority (e.g. a hospital or care home) will apply to the supervisory authority (i.e. the PCT or National Assembly or local authority) for authorisation of deprivation of liberty. The supervisory authority then commissions six assessments: age; mental health; mental capacity; best interests; eligibility; and no refusals.

1. *Age.* The person must be 18 or older.
2. *Mental health.* The person needs to have a mental disorder as defined by the Mental Health Act 1983. People with no mental disorder could not be deprived of their liberty under this provision and application would have to be made to the Court of Protection.
3. *Mental capacity.* The person must lack capacity to make a decision to be accommodated in the hospital, nursing home or care home.
4. *Best Interests.* This test includes the following conditions: the person is, or is to be, a detained resident; it is in their best interests to be a detained resident; in order to prevent harm to that person it is necessary for him to be a detained resident. It also needs to be a proportionate response to the likelihood of the relevant person suffering harm, and the seriousness of that harm, for him to be a detained resident.
5. *Eligibility.* The person must not be subject to Mental Health Act compulsion. This will require a check that there is no guardianship order, Community Treatment Order, or s 17 leave based on a liability to be detained under the Mental Health Act.
6. *No refusals.* There must be no valid refusal to the decision concerning the person's residence from someone in a position of authority such as a donee of a lasting Power of Attorney or a deputy appointed by the Court of Protection.
   For someone being treated in a hospital there must be no objection from the person themselves. In these circumstances there should be an assessment carried out under the Mental Health Act.

Authorisation of deprivation of liberty

If all six conditions are met the following points apply:

- Authorisation must be in writing and include the purpose of the deprivation of liberty, the time period (max. one year), any conditions recommended by the best interests assessor, and the reasons that each of the assessment criteria are met.
- The supervisory body appoints a representative for the person (usually on the recommendation of the best interests assessor).
- Any appeals are to the Court of Protection.

References

Publications

Ashton, G., Letts, P., Oates, L. and Terrell, M. (2006) *Mental Capacity: The New Law*. Jordans.

Brown, R. (2006) *The Approved Social Worker's Guide to Mental Health Law*. Learning Matters.

Brown, R., Adshead, G. and Pollard, A. (2007) *The Approved Social Worker's Guide to Psychiatry and Medication*. Learning Matters.

Council of Europe (1950) The European Convention on Human Rights.

Department for Constitutional Affairs (2007) *Mental Capacity Act 2005; Code of Practice*. The Stationery Office.

Department of Health (2004) *Advice on the Decision of the European Court of Human Rights in the case of HL v UK (the 'Bournewood' case)* [gateway reference 4269].

Department of Health and Welsh Office (1997) *Mental Health Act 1983, Code of Practice*. HMSO.

Department of Health (2007) *Adult Protection, Care Reviews and Independent Mental Capacity Advocates (IMCA): Guidance on interpreting the regulations extending the IMCA role* [gateway reference 7557].

Harbour, A. (2008) *Mentally Disordered Children and the Law*. Jessica Kingsley.

Law Commission (1991) *Mentally Incapacitated Adults and Decision-Making. An Overview*. Consultation Paper No. 119, HMSO.

Law Commission (1995) *Mental Incapacity*. Law Com No. 231.

Law Society (1989) *Decision-making and Mental Incapacity: A Discussion Document*. Memorandum by the Law Society's Mental Health Sub-Committee.

Lord Chancellor's Department (1997) *Who Decides? Making Decisions on Behalf of Mentally Incapacitated Adults*. Cm 3803.

Lord Chancellor's Department (1999) *Making Decisions*. Cm 4465.

Martin, E. and Law, J. (Eds) (2006) *Oxford Dictionary of Law*. Oxford University Press.

Montgomery, J. (2002) *Health Care Law*. Oxford University Press.

Puri, B., Brown, R., McKee, H. and Treasaden, I. (2005) *Mental Health Law*. Hodder Arnold.

Statutes

1948 National Assistance Act

1969 Family Law Reform Act

1976 and 2000 Race Relations Acts

1977 National Health Service Act

1983 Mental Health Act

1984 Police and Criminal Evidence Act

1985 Enduring Powers of Attorney Act

1989 Children Act

1990 National Health Service and Community Care Act

1998 Human Rights Act

1999 Health Act

2005 Mental Capacity Act

2007 Mental Health Act

Regulations and Statutory Instruments

Court of Protection Fees Order (SI 2007, No. 1745)

Court of Protection Rules (SI 2007, No. 1744)

Lasting Powers of Attorney, Enduring Powers of Attorney and Public Guardian Regulations (SI 2007, No. 1253).

Mental Capacity Act 2005 (Independent Mental Capacity Advocates) (Expansion of Role) Regulations (SI 2006, No. 2883)

Mental Capacity Act 2005 (Independent Mental Capacity Advocates) (General) Regulations (SI 2006, No. 1832)

Mental Capacity Act 2005 (Loss of Capacity during Research Project) (England) Regulations (SI 2007, No. 679)

Mental Capacity Act 2005 (Transfer of Proceedings) Order (SI 2007, No. 1899)

Mental Capacity Act 2005 (Transitional and Consequential Provisions) Order 2007 (SI 2007 No. 1898)

Public Guardian (Fees etc.) Regulations (SI 2007, No. 2051)

Cases

Airedale NHS Trust v Bland [1993] 2 WLR 316

Bird v Luckie (1850) 8 Hare 301

C, Re (Adult: Refusal of Medical Treatment) [1994] 1 WLR 290

HL v UK (2005) 40 EHRR 32 (the Bournewood case)

JE v DE (1), Surrey CC (2) [2006] EWHC 3549 (Fam) (deprivation of liberty)

R v Ashworth Hospital (now Mersey Care NHS Trust), ex p Munjaz [2005] 3 WLR 793

T, Re (Adult Refusal of Medical Treatment) [1992] 4 All ER 649

Some useful websites

Public Guardianship Office	**www.guardianship.gov.uk**
Ministry of Justice	**www.justice.gov.uk**

(this used to be the Department of Constitutional Affairs on **www.dca.gov.uk**) and booklets are at **www.dca.gov.uk/legal-policy/mental-capacity/publications.htm**

Department of Health	**www.doh.gov.uk**
Welsh Assembly	**www.wales.gov.uk**
Mental Health Act Commission	**www.mhac.org.uk**
Mental health law (IMHAP site)	**www.imhap.org.uk**

Index